A HOUSE ON THE WATER

Inspiration for Living at the Water's Edge

A HOUSE ON THE WATER

Robert Knight

Photography by Randy O'Rourke

The Taunton Press

The Taunton Press, Inc., 63 South Main Street, PO Box 5506, Newtown, CT 06470-5506
e-mail: tp@taunton.com

Distributed by Publishers Group West

Editor: Peter Chapman
Interior design: Lori Wendin
Layout: Lori Wendin
Illustrator: Christine Erikson
Photographer: Randy O'Rourke

A House on the Water was originally published in hardcover
in 2003 by The Taunton Press, Inc.

Library of Congress Cataloging-in-Publication Data
Knight, Robert, 1944-
   A house on the water : inspiration for living at the water's edge /
Robert Knight.
        p. cm.
   ISBN 1-56158-607-2 hardcover
   ISBN 1-56158-744-3 paperback
   1. Seaside architecture--New England. 2. Lakeside architecture--New
England. 3. Architecture, Domestic--New England. I. Title.
   NA7575.K58 2003
   728'.0974'09146--dc21
                        2003009032

Printed in the United States of America
10 9 8 7 6 5 4 3 2 1

The following manufacturers/names appearing in *A House on the Water* are trademarks: Kevlar®, Fireslate®

Acknowledgments

*To my best friend Lucia, who started me writing
and will always be my first editor*

I AM INDEBTED TO TWO ARCHITECTS who shaped the way I see the world: the late Charles W. Moore, who taught me in school and out, and David Marshall, who has always known what is important. In addition, I'd like to extend my thanks to all the people who helped with the creation of this book:

Peter Chapman, my editor at The Taunton Press, who edited and coached me through this book from start to finish. By the end he was changing little, and we can't figure out if it was because I started to sound more like him or he began to sound more like me. Thanks also to everyone else on the Taunton book team, including Jim Childs, Paula Schlosser, Wendi Mijal, Carol Singer, Robyn Doyon-Aitken, illustrator Christine Erikson, and book designer Lori Wendin. And a special thanks to Kevin Ireton of *Fine Homebuilding* magazine, who started me writing for Taunton several years ago, and to Steve Culpepper, who first approached me with this project.

Randy O'Rourke (and his family), who followed me around the country taking the gorgeous photographs that are the real reason you bought this book. He was always cheerfully willing to wait the extra day or come back and take the boat out again when the light was better to get the impossible shots that I asked for.

My wife, Lucia, who kept the office running and was always willing to be the first editor of my copy even as she neared the end of her own writing project, *The Encyclopedia of Yacht Designers.*

My architectural partner, Peter d'Entremont, who with quiet good humor put up with the tremendous amount of time I spent on this project and filled in for me so we didn't go under.

My office manager, B. G. Thorpe, who became a "clerk of the works" on this project, keeping records up to date and mailing things on time to the right place. I would have been lost without her.

I visited all the homes featured in this book, and in many cases the architects took a lot of time out of their schedules to show me around. I thank them all, with special mention to Max Jacobson (and his daughter), who showed up on Father's Day morning—way above and beyond the call of duty.

Peter Bohlin, who was especially supportive over the phone and gave me lots of hours of his staff's time as well. In the lakeside house that Peter designed in Montana, Don Moffat, the job super for Martel Construction, took the best part of a day showing me around. He was a great guide and would be the guy any architect would want building his best houses.

Heartfelt thanks to Tom and Sally Reeve, for giving me the run of their wonderful house in the San Juan Islands, and to all the other homeowners who went out of their way so I could understand their homes. And a special mention to Captain George Cole, who spent days driving Randy (and me) around in his boat so we could shoot the four houses around Penobscot Bay.

CONTENTS

INTRODUCTION

LAND AT THE WATER'S EDGE is different—it's where two worlds meet, where weather systems collide, where views are longer, and where you can almost feel as though you own a little piece of infinity. This difference at the water's edge can help you build a great house that improves its site and your life—but it's also something of a public trust. Just as building on a neighborhood street has its obligations, building a house on the water requires respect for the public space that surrounds it. A waterside home gives great rewards, but it demands care in return.

I live on the coast of Maine and spend whatever time I can sailing along the water. Because I'm an architect, I find myself looking at the architecture as much as the scenery. From the water, lots of old houses seem to complement the landscape, to complete a picture, but many of the newer homes are strangely orphaned from their surroundings, ill at ease on this glorious coastline.

If you've always dreamed of living at the water's edge, perhaps you are thinking of something different—of creating a home that does feel like it belongs in its setting, a home that not only enhances your life but also the coastline itself.

Good house design is the result of a complex interaction between site, designer, and client. It's not possible to lay out a recipe from one house that will guarantee success with another, but there are recurring themes that are effective in making a house work well in any waterside setting—design themes that deal with siting, scale, room layout, and use of materials that apply to any style of house.

A big part of designing buildings by the water is coping with unique construction challenges that come with being on the margin—sloping sites, high winds, lots of moisture in the air, corrosion from salt, and different impacts from the sun than are experienced on inland sites. Good houses on the coast deal with these issues successfully, and the solutions to these technical problems enhance the quality of the design rather than forcing compromises in it.

When I was in college, my freehand drawing teacher told the class that if we worked very hard, in a year a few of us would learn how to draw (I didn't), but that all of us would definitely learn what a good drawing was and how to recognize it. And we did, because he taught us how to see in new ways. Similarly, it's not necessary to learn how to design a great house on the water—there are plenty of good architects you can hire. But it is extremely useful to be able to see the possibilities of something good and rec-

ognize it when it starts to take shape so you can encourage it in the right direction. My hope is that this book will take you an amiable way along that road.

Whether you are actively creating a home at the water's edge or simply dreaming about it, I hope *A House on the Water* will provide both inspiration and valuable design advice for a home that respects the coastline, fits into the surroundings, and is built to withstand the unique conditions of the site for generations to come.

Creating a portal to the dunes and the beach beyond, this house on Martha's Vineyard lives in intimate contact with the waterfront.

At the WATER'S EDGE

I HAVE STOOD BY THE WATER with many clients and shared the excitement they feel about building a house at the edge of land. Living on the water is an almost universal desire, whether it's a house on the beach, high on a cliff, beside a lake, or overlooking a river or stream. But it hasn't always been that way.

Many of the houses that feel at home along the coast have been there for 100 years or more. The people who built these original homes weren't necessarily dreaming of a house on the water. They worked outside, doing demanding physical labor: fishing, farming, mining, logging. After a 12-hour day exposed to the elements, they sought shelter in their homes—even shelter from the view—having "participated" with the water all day. Consequently, houses built in the 1800s were mostly about walls, and in large part they turned their backs on the water. Windows were to admit light and fresh air, and outside views were incidental, almost avoided by planned intent.

Today, by contrast, most people living on the water have occupations that keep them inside. In their homes, especially if they have gone to the trouble and expense of buying waterfront property, they want to experience the water as much as possible. Building a house on the water where

Balancing views to the water against the need for privacy and a sense of security is one of the keys to a successful waterfront home.

ABOVE | *In houses built over a hundred years ago, shelter was more important than view in making choices about windows.*

BELOW | *The wide wall of windows looking down to the ocean almost makes it seem as though the kitchen is more outside than inside.*

walls are more important than windows won't satisfy today's owners because it won't fulfill the need to be connected to the outdoors.

Creating a house that "belongs" requires learning the design concepts from the past and adding new components that address current lifestyle needs. At first glance, a new house on the water may look a great deal like an old house, but it will have a very different floor plan. It man have window that look like they came from the 19th century, but they will be used in a different way. Or the new house may look very different in style, roofline, or use of materials but in fact exhibit the same skillful use of scale, siting, and a sympathy to the waterfront that made those old houses work so well.

The Response to the Water

Great houses grow out of the fruitful interaction among architect, client, and site. When the site is at the water's edge, the relationship of the building to the water is always one of the critical elements in this interaction. Each of the houses presented in this book has a different response to its particular waterfront site, but the architects who designed them used similar conceptual tools to create these very different houses. Giving names to those tools lends an insight into the design process, which will make it more rewarding if you are going to build or buy a house on the waterfront or if you just want to enjoy what somebody else has created. Here are the six key design tools:

○ **A SENSE OF FITTING IN:** All the issues of siting and massing that make a successful house appear to be "the right design in the right place."

○ **THE EXPERIENCE OF APPROACH:** The paths that bring us to the house, from land and from water, that predetermine how we experience the house and what we expect of it.

○ **BALANCING LOOKING IN** and **LOOKING OUT:** How views are managed and framed, both outside looking in and inside looking out.

Even in this interior room, there's an imaginary path (or "axis") out to the water, drawing our attention to it. The zinnias on the table are lined up along the path.

○ **CREATING GRACIOUS TRANSITIONS:** Creating indoor/outdoor spaces, such as decks, porches, patios, alcoves, breezeways, courtyards, and sometimes just the space between a cluster of buildings.

○ **SHAPING INTERIOR SPACES:** Using the organization of spaces, ceiling heights, scale tricks, and other tools to create a cohesive interior design that makes the most of where and what the house is.

○ **COMPOSING THE ELEMENTS:** How the actual parts that make up the building—windows, doors, roofs, floors, and all their embellishments—are used to wed the house to the site.

A Sense of Fitting In

How well a house fits its site and relates to the water is the most important factor in determining the success of a waterfront home. Fitting in can mean trying to be unobtrusive, or even invisible, but more often it is a question of complementing or completing a picture, so that it feels as though the site has always been waiting for just that house. There are a number of ways to fit in with the landscape, depending on the type of architecture and the kind of land available.

Floating like a grass bridge across the gap in the cliff face, the sod roof of this northwest-coast house is a simple but powerful form that feels at home on this dramatic site without dominating it.

The strong composition of the elements of this lakeside house complements the dark backdrop of the trees. The contrast completes the picture.

COMPLEMENTING

Even a small house, if it has a certain formal or geometric presence, can lay visual claim to a large piece of shoreline to good effect. The trick lies in getting the house to appear to complete the site, to anchor everything to it. For example, the Muskoka boathouse shown at left (and on pp. 132–139) is a small building, but there's a strong sense that this piece of lakefront would be missing something if it wasn't there.

Fitting in by complementing what's there is the most difficult of site strategies to pull off gracefully, and abusing it has resulted in some ugly buildings that are spectacularly noticeable. If the land and the building do not work together in this effort, you end up with a building that shouts loudly for attention when it would be better off not getting any.

MERGING

To merge with the landscape, a house must echo the natural forms and either disappear (sometimes literally) or, more often, sympathize with the site, acting like a partner in a dance. On rough sites with dramatic, demanding topography, where competing with the drama of the site would be counterproductive, merging a powerful form can also bring a sense of completion, as with the house Jim Cutler put in the notch of a cliff on the Pacific Northwest coast (see the top photo on the facing page and pp. 150–159). Because these dramatic sites are often naturally beautiful, it's important that a house built there weave into the fabric of the site very subtly so that it changes the dynamic only minimally.

Fitting in with surrounding architecture is largely a matter of rhythm, scale, massing, and sympathetic detailing, rather than slavishly imitating design details of neighboring structures. Indeed, the strict imitation often insisted upon by design review boards almost always falls flat, seeming somehow off key, because it is copying the past rather than looking for the spirit of the neighborhood. When you look at a row of houses along the shore you should feel that a visual rhythm is being completed, as it is in the house on Bainbridge Island designed by Peter Manning (see the photo at right and pp. 160–169). What you don't want to experience is "beep beep bop beep bop bop BUMP beep bop…."

With just a few straight lines showing above a veil of greenery, this house in Montana is almost invisible from the water.

On some waterfront sites, the rhythm and scale of the neighboring buildings are the dominant themes that must be addressed for a house to fit in.

SCALE, PROPORTION, AND MASSING

When we talk about "fitting in," there are three main factors that come into play: scale, proportion, and massing.

Scale is a factor of the size of the building and its components relative to other site features—and relative to human size. A house with "no scale," a phrase often used by architects, usually means there is no visual way of assessing how big the building really is because there are no reliable clues to relate to. For example, a house with all oversized windows and doors may give very misleading information about how big it really is. Sometimes this is used skillfully to create a unique house (as shown in the photo at right), but more often it is a mistake and makes one feel uneasy.

Proportion is related to scale, but a house might be quite well proportioned relative to itself, but out of proportion with the site elements.

Massing is the overall impact of the house form, relative to the site and other nearby forms. It is the size and shape of the building. For example, a large blocklike house needs a lot of visual space to sit comfortably. If it is very close to visual borders to the site—or to other house that seem to create a border—it will probably look ungainly.

This house on the Maine coast blocks the view of the water on the entry side (above). Once inside, the view opens up as the entry foyer expands into the two-story space of the living room (top).

The Experience of Approach

How we approach a house, both with our eyes and our feet, has a lot to do with how we eventually judge it. First impressions are critical, and the expectations created on the approach in large part shape how we subsequently feel about the house.

Some houses reveal themselves only when we enter, surprising us with great interior drama or powerful views that we hadn't expected. This sudden drama makes the house unforgettable. Other houses maintain an incremental low-key personality, eschewing drama for a more contemplative beauty that reveals itself slowly over time.

One of the biggest challenges when designing a house on the water is that there are two very different approaches to the house: one from the land and one from the water. Unlike a house on a street, where the approach is totally controlled and is always on the same side, a house on the water has an approach from the land that is usually on the opposite side from the approach from the water. As a practical matter, many waterfront homes do not have an actual approach from the water—such as a boat landing—but they all need to deal with the fact that they are seen in a formal manner from the water, so they have to possess two "fronts."

Of course, "the experience of approach" has a big impact on "fitting in." There's overlap in all of these themes, and it doesn't work to try to put everything in a neat box. These categories should be used more as memory aids than as formulas—for example, I don't know any good designer who ever sat down and said, "Let's claim this ocean view."

Balancing Looking In and Looking Out

Looking into a house is a sequel to how the house is approached. It adds another layer of drama to see through to the water from the entry. In the house Jim Estes designed on Narragansett Bay (see the top photo on p. 12 and pp. 20–27), as you approach the front door you can see right through to the bay and the entry frames your first view of the water. Looking into the house makes you want to go inside. In the house in the San Juan islands (see the bottom photo on p. 12 and pp. 150–159), Jim Cutler created passage through the house to glimpse a great long-distance view, but the inside of the house remains a mystery.

When looking out of a house, windows and door openings frame and shape the view. The "looking out" aspect always needs to be balanced against an equivalent need for a sense of shelter and protection in this somewhat hostile environment at the boundary between land and water. Views need to be framed to remind us of the security that the house is giving us. We need to feel this security in order to allow ourselves to be immersed in the view. It's like the security of a railing at the edge of cliff that allows you to approach the edge.

How views of land and water are controlled from within the house shapes our perception of both the land and

Dealing with the landward approach to a coastal home (above) is often the most difficult design challenge, because the house is "looking" in the other direction (top).

TOP LEFT | *The approach to this house reveals the transparency of the water side, drawing us inside—but with a pause on the welcoming porch first.*

BOTTOM LEFT | *Here, the house is opaque, but the powerful notch in the wall acts as a magnet that draws us through the house to the distant view of the mountains.*

water outside and the house itself. For example, consciously lowering head height on dormer windows under the eaves of a low roof pulls your vision down to the water or land instead of straight out, while dramatically changing the sense of scale in the room.

The types of windows used influence our perception of looking out. For example, a window with muntin bars (thin strips of wood that divide the window) increases the sense of containment in a room, whereas a single pane, or "light," of glass looks out without restraint but decreases our sense of security. This subtle difference affects how people live in the house and interact with the outside.

These same muntins, or lack of them, have a profound effect on how people perceive the house from the outside. Whereas muntins maintain the continuity of the skin of the structure, large single-light windows may look like painful holes punched through the skin unless the composition of the whole design supports them. The cottage on Martha's Vineyard (see the top photo on p. 14 and pp. 20–27) would look quite ill at ease without muntin bars, whereas in the

Large, single-light windows are appropriate to the scale and design of this house. The sense of the wall as a thin screen against the weather is emphasized by the lack of trim and the delicacy of the wall of windows.

How much you use an exterior deck can be strongly influenced by the view looking back into the house from the deck. The outdoor living room in this Maine house would be a lot less comfortable without the sense of being embraced by the house.

RIGHT | *The gently curved porch leads from a quiet garden on the sheltered side of the house out to an open deck on the waterfront.*

BELOW | *The rhythm of large sheets of glass works well with the simple lines of this house. Here, windows with multiple panes would look out of place.*

Windows with smaller panes maintain the visual integrity of the skin of the house. They are also in keeping with the delicacy of the trim and shingle lines.

house designed by Obie Bowman in northern California (see the photo at left and pp. 176–183) the large single-light windows establish a very comfortable scale.

Creating Gracious Transitions

As pointed out earlier, most people who build by the water make their living working inside, and in their leisure time they typically want to experience the water as much as possible. Instead of the black and white transition from inside to outside that characterized 19th-century waterfront homes, successful houses today will often have transitional spaces that are neither totally inside nor out. These spaces create a gray zone between black and white, interior and exterior, encouraging us to come as far out of our shelter as weather will allow.

Stepping out onto a screened porch, you are still contained by walls and roof, although the walls are porous. Going further, to a porch with no screening, still gives you the shelter of a roof, the definition of columns, and probably a railing. The next level of exposure is a deck with no roof over it and minimal containment at the edge.

Screened porch, deck, and pergola combine to create layers of transition from inside to out on this Martha's Vineyard beach house.

One step back from an open deck is one covered with a pergola. In places where the shading effect of a roof would darken the inside of the house too much, a pergola of open beams above the deck allows you to feel the protection of the house reaching out around you, changes the scale so a high wall behind may not be so imposing, and gives another shade of gray along the inside-outside continuum. These transitional spaces can also increase the sense of protection from a harsh exterior by creating a visual, psychological, and sometimes real buffer to the environment.

Shaping Interior Spaces

Dealing with interior space is the most "right brained" or intuitive part of the design process because it is the most complex. How three-dimensional spaces inside a house are

A false wall and pergola frame a transitional space that encourages movement from inside the house to outside on this roof deck in California.

A walled garden makes an effective outdoor living room on the protected entry side, away from the harsher conditions on the water side.

proportioned, shaped, and organized determines whether a house is an enjoyable place to live.

Architects work from a client's wish list: how many bedrooms, bathrooms, closets, and so on, a house should have. From that shopping list, the architect needs to shape spaces that are comfortable for the purposes intended and that relate to each other functionally and visually. In a waterfront home, a critical part of that spatial management is the relationship to the water views, the path of the sun and the direction of prevailing winds (see the drawing on the facing page). Integrating this added dimension, without it fighting with the spaces or overwhelming the inside of the house, is one of the subtlest and most difficult parts of designing a house on the water.

Running a wide molding around the room just above door height gives this large barnlike space a more comfortable domestic scale.

All the rooms in this lakeside house are laid out with a view of the water. Here, the main living space flows out to the deck overlooking the lake.

Room layouts should respond to the views and to the location of the sun and encourage you to move through the house and use the rooms in different ways at different times of the day. For example, in the Maine climate that I live in, I usually try to position a screened porch on the northwest side of the house to take advantage of where the sun sets in summer.

Composing the Elements

For a house to feel wedded to its site, it must respond positively to the challenges of the site. It does this with the actual pieces of the building—roofs, walls, doors, and windows—elements that make the house watertight, safe, and practical, but also comfortable, exciting, and beautiful. These might be a deep roof overhang, which shades the

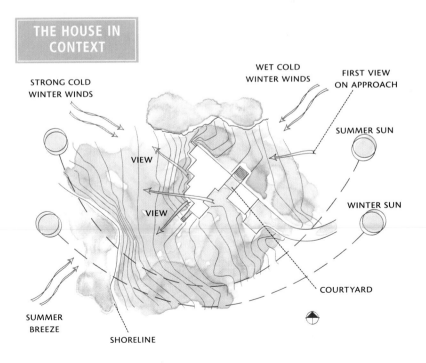

THE HOUSE IN CONTEXT

STRONG COLD WINTER WINDS

WET COLD WINTER WINDS

FIRST VIEW ON APPROACH

SUMMER SUN

VIEW

VIEW

WINTER SUN

COURTYARD

SUMMER BREEZE

SHORELINE

RIGHT | *Extending the stacked planks from an intersecting wall creates a screen and gives this modest house a different visual dimension with very little effort.*

BELOW | *The dynamic planes of roof and walls are a striking composition of abstract elements, as much sculpture as "house."*

interior from strong sun and glare from the water while at the same time making the roof appear to hover over the house, or landscape devices like stairs and stone walls that change the scale of the house relative to the land.

While creating the pieces that make up the actual house is important in its own right, these pieces are also the result of thinking about all the other themes we have already talked about. Detailing falls into this category. Mies van der Rohe, modernism's most sublime advocate, is often quoted as having said, "God is in the details," but I tend to think that a building's soul is in the spaces, rhythms, and light within a building. If it isn't there, the detailing will just seem pretty and overdone. Good detailing, however, echoes the larger themes of the house and encourages us to look closer without losing the sense of the whole.

On the shore, keeping the water on the outside of the building often calls for unusual construction details and methods. In a great design, the architect will take advantage of these stringent requirements to create elements that visually echo the demands that the site is making on the building. Good historical examples of this are the gar-

The steel band strength that allows this wall of glass to withstand high winds, at the same time makes the wall seem more delicate.

goyles that adorn gothic cathedrals. To keep the water that comes off the roof from running down the limestone walls of the cathedral and rapidly eroding them, the architects needed to shoot the water out into space, so they created these mythical monsters that spat the water out; they took advantage of a problem and created a new form that now seems to have its own reason for being.

Each of the houses presented on the pages that follow deals successfully with all the above issues, but I will focus on the most prominent aspects of each house. Nametags are useful to navigate through new territory and to facilitate talking about what the photographs show, but the best way to understand why these houses are good is to look hard at the photographic evidence and let the part of your brain that doesn't name things take over.

The entry porch on the sheltered landward side of the house reaches out to greet visitors and gives a strong sense of the transparency of the waterside wall.

Natural materials, subtle shifts in scale, and terrific waterfront views combine to produce a house of seemingly effortless refinement. Sitting quietly on the Rhode Island shore, the house looks as though it has always been there.

A QUIET FIT

IF EVER A HOUSE LOOKED like it belonged on its site, this is it. From the water, the house is so quiet and restrained that you might sail right on by without noticing it . . . or if you did, think, "Yes, that house has always been there." And that's the intent.

Architect Jim Estes (of Estes/Twombly Architects) has created a house on Narragansett Bay in Rhode Island that is the simplest of ideas in terms of shapes and room layout. Its style is an updated version of the traditional shingled houses found along the shore in this part of the country. What sets the house apart is not a bravura style or radical floor plan but the extremely skillful crafting of the pieces of the house and the subtle ways they are fitted together.

Emphasizing the delicacy of the stonework, the cherry mantel's curving back is recessed into the small Pennsylvania stones.

Separated from the living room by the stone fireplace, the kitchen is a cozier, more intimate space under a low, flat ceiling. The balcony above is used as a study.

Point of Arrival

The approach to a house sets up a certain expectation of what is to come—or it should. The approach to this house is a classic example of setting up and fulfilling those expectations.

The driveway passes through a screen of birch trees before arriving at a slate and pebble-floored courtyard that leads to the covered entry. On this, the landward side of the house, exterior spaces are sheltered from the glare and winds off the water. The entry itself has a sheltering roof and a pair of built-in benches that encourage you to pause a moment before going inside. With curved armrests and roof brackets above, the entry porch has the feel of a welcoming inglenook (without the fireplace). The interior layout is a direct response to the waterfront site, with the principal daytime rooms (living, eating, kitchen) spread out in a line from north to south looking out over the water. Bedrooms are in a separate two-story bunkhouse wing to the north of the living room.

Adjusting the Scale

When you enter a modestly sized house it's always a pleasant surprise when the main living space feels spacious, but not overwhelming. This one is just right. One reason for

SITE PLAN

SUMMER WINDS

WINTER WINDS

ABOVE | *In the living room, the massive stone fireplace balances the transparency of the floor-to-ceiling window wall, while the rich wood tones of the exposed ceiling lend a comforting warmth to a two-story space.*

LEFT | *Late afternoon sun brings out the rich hues of the cedar-shingled walls and roof that have said "home" to generations of New Englanders.*

Stone steps built into the fireplace wall provide the only way up to the study loft, a striking contrast to the gentler rise of the traditional stairway beyond, which leads to the second-story bedrooms.

this is the scale of the floor-to-ceiling double-hung windows on the east facade. Because they are larger than standard-size windows, you might expect them to make the room seem bigger, but the opposite is true—they make this largest room in the house seem more human-sized and comfortable.

To the right of the living room, the kitchen, tucked under a balcony beyond the central stone fireplace, draws us to the sunny end of the house. Here, in the room where the owners spend much of their time, Estes has made a couple of subtle adjustments to take advantage of the best views in the house. First, the window wall is bent into a gentle V-shaped bay, like a modified ship's prow, which gives focus to the views and also creates a well-defined spot for the dining table. Second, the roof over the kitchen/dining area is raised about 1 ft., which means that the overhanging eaves are higher than in the living room, opening up more of the view. Raising the roof also adds just enough height to create a cozy workspace under the eaves on the second-floor balcony. From the exterior, staggering the roof height makes the house look like a composition of pieces rather than one big unified shape. The house becomes more intimate and welcoming, but it is so subtly done that you don't notice it at first glance.

FIRST FLOOR PLAN

ENTRY

BEDROOM

STUDY

KITCHEN

LIVING ROOM

DINING ROOM

BEDROOM

STAIRS TO STUDY LOFT

A dormer in the low-roofed study above the kitchen provides the necessary headroom and a view over the gardens at the back of the house.

The wall of the dining room opens out into a shallow V-shaped bay window, intensifying the focus on the view and giving stronger definition to the eating space.

The Central Fireplace

The focal point of the house is the massive stone fireplace, which both anchors the floor plan and casually divides the kitchen/dining area from the living room. With such a large masonry mass, there's a risk that it might overpower the room. But, once again, Estes has adjusted the scale, using a small stone from Pennsylvania rather than larger rocks. He further emphasized the delicacy of the stone by slightly recessing the curved cherry mantelpiece into the stone itself, making the wall seem much lighter. Estes also used the fireplace wall to provide unique access to the

A curved porch on the south side shades the hottest part of the house and leads around to a sheltered patio on the entry side.

study loft above. Rather than eating up a lot of floor space with a separate stair, he incorporated a steep stone ship's ladder into the wall itself (see the top photo on p. 24). Although it looks a little intimidating, the ladder is actually easy to climb, and the unusual act of getting up there emphasizes the privacy and distinctiveness of the study above.

"Cranking the Box"

The somewhat more prosaic spaces of the bedrooms are expressed more simply than the daytime living areas. Here, the rooms have standard ceiling heights (about 8 ft.), and each room has an identical boxlike layout within the bigger box of the bedroom wing.

"Cranking" (to Estes's term) the box 30 degrees off the axis of the rest of the building serves to separate it more and add a note of whimsy. This change in organization is another factor that allows us to see the pieces of the composition, making the building feel smaller and more intimate. The shift is just enough to notice, but not enough that it shouts for attention.

At the opposite end of the house a wonderful curve in the porch creates swooping shadows and leads around to the quiet gardens with river-stone paths on the sheltered western side of the house. Here, under a garden pergola, you can finish the day away from the harsher waterfront, still cooled by the southwest breezes of a summer afternoon. As the shadows lengthen, this house that's so quietly elegant slips back into the fabric of the Rhode Island waterfront. ∽

Sunshades on the corner of the bedroom wing (at right) echo the large roof overhangs that shade the large double-hung windows on this east-facing side of the house.

Corner windows and a low window seat frame the view from this first-floor bedroom, while the sunshades outside keep out the high hot sun of summer.

WHAT STYLE IS IT?

Clad from roof to foundation in red cedar shingles, this dignified Rhode Island house clearly has some of its roots in the Shingle style of architecture, made popular by such architects as H. H. Richardson and McKim, Mead, and White. This style was in vogue over a fairly short period of time, roughly between 1880 and 1900 with some spillover at either end. At the peak of the Shingle style, the large amounts of trim and often-fussy details of the Queen Anne period that preceded it had almost disappeared, giving way instead to buildings in which you can almost feel the volume inside stretching out their skin.

The Shingle style is largely an architecture of coastal areas of New England and the mid-Atlantic states, but it's a mistake to see any shingled coastal building as directly growing out of this style. This house designed by architect Jim Estes certainly has a lot of antecedents in the 19th century, but the distinctive overhanging eyebrows over the window are more typical of the slightly earlier Stick Style. The simple rectangular volumes of this house also owe more to the farmhouse vernacular architecture of this region than to the Shingle style. Let's just call it "Shingle style, evolved."

With a stucco facade, simple window shapes, and minimal trim, the house has a restrained presence at the water's edge.

BETWEEN THE GARDEN AND THE BAY

THIS SIMPLE, RECTANGULAR HOUSE, renovated by architect Cass Calder Smith, sits on a tight waterfront lot, perched between a wonderful private entry garden on the landward side and San Francisco Bay to the west. In many Bay Area towns, the houses along the water crowd out all views of the water, and any sense of a building or its occupants is mostly of double-wide garage doors, relieved by occasional splashes of tropical greenery. But this house stands out from its one- and two-story neighbors in that it serves as a graceful bridge between land and water rather than an imposing barrier.

The doors to the central hallway open wide, providing a direct connection between the water and the private garden on the landward side. A slatted wooden arbor above the far doors shades the west-facing dining room from the high summer sun.

A raised planter brimming with flowers and foliage, an olive tree, and a pergola frame the entry gate, distinguishing this house from the garage-dominated fronts along the rest of the street.

A Strong Entry

The first thing that sets this stucco-faced house apart from its neighbors is that it has a real entrance. A beautiful flower-covered planter, an olive tree, and a pergola frame the entry gate, helping to push the understated garage into the background. Opening the gate places you on a path directly through the house to the water. Paths like these, or "axes" as they are called in architectural jargon, are the organizational focus for the house.

To create a strong connection between the garden and the water, Smith laid out the first floor of the house as three long rooms that stretch between them. There's a combination living and dining room on one end, a kitchen and family eating area on the other, and a hallway and staircase in between. Each room has identical openings on the garden and water side. With neighboring houses to the north and south, all the orientation of this house is east to the garden or west to the water. Inside the house, you'd hardly know the neighbors are only a few feet away.

As a result of the strong connections, the house seems balanced between the drama of the water view (and Mt. Tamalpais in the distance) and the closer, more private world of the garden. On warm, sunny days, the windows and doors on the waterside can be thrown open to the deck, but on days when the weather turns windy and hostile (all too often in these parts), the house can turn its back on the water and focus inward on the sheltering garden of olive trees and flowers.

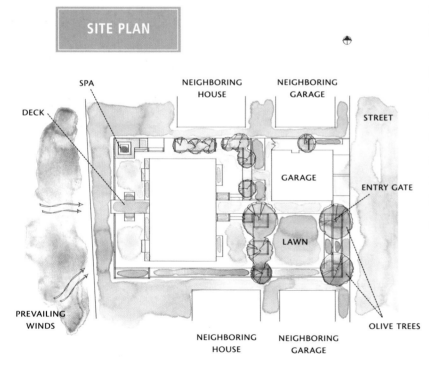

SITE PLAN

DECK

SPA

NEIGHBORING HOUSE

NEIGHBORING GARAGE

STREET

GARAGE

ENTRY GATE

LAWN

PREVAILING WINDS

NEIGHBORING HOUSE

NEIGHBORING GARAGE

OLIVE TREES

A paved path along the north side of the house reinforces the sense of connection between garden and water.

With the entry gate open, there's a direct view through the house to the water and
Mt. Tamalpais beyond.

The exterior space is organized into areas bounded by low walls, limestone paving, and manicured lawns. The mature olive trees offer some free-form contrast to this ordered environment.

An Outdoor Living Room

The sense of order on the inside of the house is extended to the garden, where low walls framing limestone-paved walks, a manicured lawn, and large potted trees define this space as an outdoor living room. The limestone paving of the garden flows around the house, ending in the deck at the water's edge. These paved side paths increase the sense of passage and connection between the garden and the water. When the doors at the ends of the three house passages are open, the house itself, understated with a combination of minimalist detailing and flat stuccoed walls, seems more like a resting point between the water and greenery than a destination in itself.

Formal Places, Casual Spaces

The interior layout and furnishings of the house are a study in contrasts. The living and dining room on the south side are used primarily for entertaining, with traditional furniture that sets a decidedly formal tone. By contrast, the large kitchen and family area on the north side of the house are much more casual. Here, contemporary furniture is integrated into a very functional work and play space. The central hallway provides a direct connection between water and garden without disrupting either living space and functions as a buffer between the two zones.

A skylight along the south wall of the house brings in balancing light and maintains the privacy of the living and dining room from the neighboring house, which is only a few feet away.

FIRST FLOOR PLAN

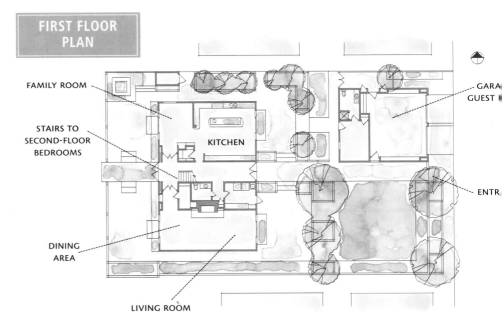

FAMILY ROOM

STAIRS TO SECOND-FLOOR BEDROOMS

KITCHEN

DINING AREA

LIVING ROOM

GARA
GUEST

ENTR

ABOVE | *Looking back through the house from the water toward the entry gate gives a strong sense of this house's "through-axis" organization. The stairs lead to the three second-floor bedrooms.*

LEFT | *Large doors from the family room establish a strong connection with the water. An identical opening on the facing wall connects the kitchen to the garden.*

A thicker wall in the west-facing dining room allows the large roll-up shades to be hidden from view when not in use.

This is a great layout for an action-oriented family with young children. The kids can zoom through the house, maybe with a quick pit stop in the kitchen, as they go from the comforting surrounds of the garden out to the water-side deck and the attractions of hot tub, swimming, and boating. The south side of the house is spared all this activity and remains a more formal oasis between garden and water.

Controlling the Light

It's hard to imagine that there is one, but one drawback of living in a house on the water with a west-facing exposure is that the sun can be overpowering at the height of summer. Good sun control must be built into the house. Here, a pair of slatted wood arbors extends out over the doors to the dining room and the informal eating area, providing shade from the high summer sun (see the photo on p. 29). On days when even the low western sun is too hot, ceiling-to-floor shades can be lowered to block the sun. The walls on this side of the house are thicker to accommodate the shades, and when they are rolled up they disappear completely. ∽

On the south side of the house, doors from the garden lead into the composed and formal world of the living room and dining room.

The family side of the house to the north is more casual, with contemporary cabinetry and functional furniture setting an informal tone.

The interior is a restrained palette of materials, with plain white walls playing off the limestone floor, natural wood, and the glass-faced upper cabinets.

LIGHT FROM ABOVE

On tight waterfront lots where there are adjacent houses on either side, it's not desirable to have windows on the side walls for reasons of privacy. But it is, of course, desirable to get light into the middle of the house.

To meet this challenge, architect Cass Calder Smith recessed the second-floor walls of this house by about 4 ft. so he could put skylights over the first floor

at the edges of the house. These two skylights wash the living/dining area and the kitchen with natural light. He installed a third skylight over the central hallway, which adds to the drama and energy of this space and prevents it from looking like a long dark tunnel. This long central skylight also balances the light that comes in from the west-facing windows

on the water side and the east-facing windows onto the garden.

The skylights provide daylight even when the sun isn't shining because they reflect the light from the sky—hence the name. Because skylights let in a lot of this reflected "sky" light, even on cloudy days they are a good choice for bringing light deep into buildings and balancing strong light from large windows.

The house is visible from the water, but it doesn't overpower the coastline; it completes the picture rather than shouting for attention.

THE PERFECT SITE

WITH BEAUTIFUL OLD PASTURE OAKS and a gently sloping field that falls away to the south and overlooks a sheltered river estuary, the site for this Maine house was close to perfect. To the west, the land narrowed to a point with a spectacular view across the river to a historic Maine coastal village. To the east, more fields with large trees would shelter the owners, Adin and Heather, from their neighbor's view. Behind, and to the north, the land rose gently and turned from field to oak forest.

Ironically, building a house on a seemingly perfect lot is not without its challenges. The west-facing point was spectacular, but building on it would expose the house to the harsh northwest winter winds that come sweeping down the river. It would also mean cutting down a large number of old-

Designing a year-round home in northern climates is particularly challenging because the winters are so severe. Here, the building is spread out from east to west with broad expanses of windows to capture the low winter sun.

ABOVE | *At the main entry, the shingled walls curve outward, reaching out to draw us into the home. The custom entry door is 6 in. wider than the standard 36-in. door, which changes the scale of the entry.*

FACING PAGE | *Once inside, the low ceiling of the entry foyer gives way to the towering ceiling of the main living space.*

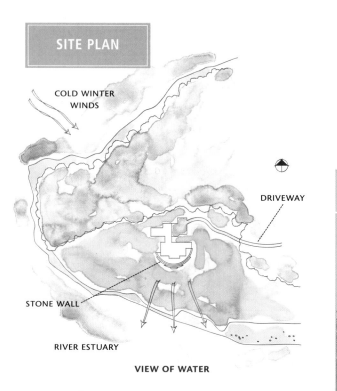

SITE PLAN

COLD WINTER WINDS

DRIVEWAY

STONE WALL

RIVER ESTUARY

VIEW OF WATER

growth oaks, and it would shout to the village across the river "here we are," which was not the impression Adin and Heather wanted to create. They knew this site was cherished locally as a beautiful unspoiled piece of land, and they wanted to build a home that would seem as if the site had been waiting for just this house to complete it.

The design of the house (by Knight Associates) was driven by three needs: to avoid the exposures of the western point, to capture winter sun in the south, and to provide shelter from the north. All the daytime rooms open to the winter sun. In winter, sunlight is limited and the sun is low in the south, so it's important that the house capture as much of that light as it can by having the rooms that are used in the daytime spread out from east to west facing south. Then the occupants can feel the progress of the sun throughout the day.

The First Glimpse of Water

One of the most exciting things about approaching a house on the water is getting that first glimpse of the water. Here, the first view is from within the woods, framed by the oaks and looking out over the field to the south. But as you get closer to the house, the view of the water is traded for a large oak tree that overhangs the entry court; the water is gone and you have to go inside the house to see it again.

NOTEBOOK   ENTER HERE

When there's more than one way into a house, it's important to let people know where they should enter. Here, there are two doors off the entry court. One door opens to a mudroom, which is for everyday use. The other door (of natural oak) is flanked by curved shingle walls, which are designed to attract the eye and draw visitors forward (see photo above). This is unquestionably the way to go in.

ABOVE | *A half-wall with columns defines the entry foyer and the living room as two separate spaces without blocking the view of the water, which is framed by a bank of windows and French doors.*

LEFT | *The kitchen is separated from the dining area by low walls that echo the curved walls of the main entry. The walls are high enough to conceal the countertop mess from the dining area but low enough to allow the cook to chat with the diners.*

Some houses reveal themselves only when you enter, surprising you with great interior drama or powerful views that aren't evident from the exterior. From the approach side, this house's low roofs and quiet finishes don't prepare you for the drama of the main space as you come out from under the lower ceiling of the entry into the high space of the living room.

Low walls and columns are used throughout this main room to separate spaces without cutting off the view to the water. The view is framed with a bank of windows and doors in the living room. Gathering together multipaned windows provides the light and focus of bigger "picture" windows without the loss of intimacy that comes from large uninterrupted sheets of glass.

Keeping this intimacy is especially important in a space that is suddenly larger. In this house, the expansiveness of the main space adds some drama and makes the surrounding lower-roofed spaces seem more intimate, but the big space is still comfortable because of the scale of the windows, the low wall with columns, the staircase, and the balcony. The granite fireplace, which is shared with the adjoining study, gives the living space another focus besides the water view.

A built-in window seat makes excellent use of a low-headroom space at the edge of the upstairs guest bedroom. And the view is the best in the house.

A small study (with its own granite fireplace) tucked in behind the main living space serves as a getaway spot for one of the owners.

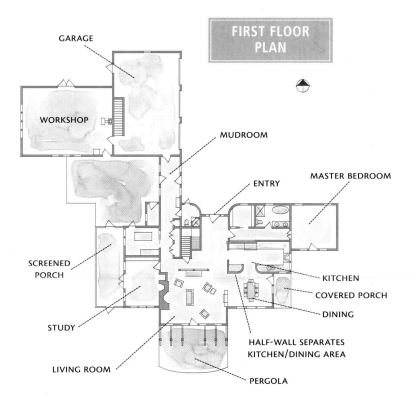

FIRST FLOOR PLAN

GARAGE

WORKSHOP

MUDROOM

ENTRY

MASTER BEDROOM

SCREENED PORCH

KITCHEN

COVERED PORCH

DINING

STUDY

HALF-WALL SEPARATES KITCHEN/DINING AREA

LIVING ROOM

PERGOLA

ABOVE | *The master bedroom is away from the main living space, down a hallway that is easily missed on first pass. Though the views from the bedroom are not as spectacular as those from upstairs, the owners make up for it with direct access to the outside and complete privacy.*

Three Gables

In terms of layout, this is an informal house, with no strict geometric organization. The relaxed layout is an intentional reflection of the way the owners like to live and also of the rambling nature of the site. However, the house needs enough compositional strength to hold its own when seen from the water—a casual collection of boxes wouldn't do.

Three strong gable dormers organize the roof structure to give the house this formal strength (see the photo on p. 37). The larger central dormer encloses the main living space, and the two flanking dormers house the upstairs guest rooms. These three triangular forms give an order to the house that makes it visually understandable,

(see the photo on p. 37)

PORCH TALK

A lot of houses on the water have open porches, screened porches, or pergolas, but this house has all three. These transition spaces encourage people to venture as far outside as the weather and bugs permit. They extend the protection of the building just a bit.

The pergola on the water side of this house serves to change the scale of the two-story facade. By putting a structure here that is more human sized—you can reach up and touch the beams—it's more comfortable to sit outside and survey one's domain. And when the domain is this good, the owners want to be out in it.

The screened porch is positioned on the western side of

but they don't put it into a strict historical style category—something the owners were keen to avoid.

Looking Out from under the Eaves

The two second-floor guestrooms are tucked tight under the eaves of the low-sloped roofs. This gives these rooms an intimate scale that is conducive to sleeping and lazing about—just what guests are supposed to do in Maine.

In the dormers facing south to the water, built-in window seats offer a great place to curl up with a book (and a view) or to put a grandchild down for a nap. There is headroom in the center of these dormers, but not on the edges, and the window seats use this space more effectively than conventional furniture. They encourage sitting (which there is headroom for), and they don't block the view the way a piece of furniture would.

Hidden in Plain Sight

While the guests have their own quarters upstairs, with the best views in the house, the owners' bedroom is hidden away on the main floor. What's going on here? Admittedly,

the owners sacrifice the longer view, but they get their own private connection to the outside, a separate deck, and complete privacy.

The door to the master suite is off the entry hall, but you don't notice it when you first go into the house because you're drawn to the larger and more brightly lit living room. From the outside as well, this wing of the house is overshadowed by the larger form of the house that draws the attention.

Tucked behind the kitchen, the master bedroom is just big enough to be comfortable, but small enough that the owners are always close to the windows, a southeastern view, and the first sun of the day. A desire for intimate contact with the land is what drew Adin and Heather to this place to begin with, and they wanted to be able to walk directly outside into the day from their bedroom.

This is a house that completes its site by fitting into the border between the woods and the field, becoming part of the edge of the water. The geometric strength of those three big gables combined with the more relaxed layout of the rest of the house creates a house that sits comfortably against the backdrop of the oak forest and doesn't compete with this exquisite site but feels like an inevitable part of it. ꙅ

the house, where the owners can enjoy the setting sun at the end of the day. It's also important to think about how a porch will shade the inside of the house. Placing this one to the west shades the interior on hot summer days but doesn't block the sun in winter, when it sets much farther to the south.

From the entry, the rich tones of the ceiling and floor finishes contrast with the smooth white walls and oiled wood trim to create a strong composition that frames the ocean view.

With its curving rooflines, the house speaks a slightly dressier, but still recognizable, language than its neighbors because the scale, height, roof pitches, and use of dormers are similar.

THE SAND BETWEEN YOUR TOES

A COTTAGE MUCH LIKE THE OTHERS along the shore had stood on this site for many years and had been rented by the present owners for about the last ten. They liked coming here, although the existing building was cut up into many tiny rooms and, to tell the truth, was not much to look at. The owners approached architect Tim Techler, who was able to get permission from the local zoning board to do a total rebuild on the same footprint, as long as the new building was smaller than the original.

The challenge was to build a new house in less square footage that would feel bigger, be rugged enough to stand up to being right on the beach, and fit in with the surrounding vernacular beachfront cottages. The lot was tiny and

ABOVE | *The porch floor decking is flush with the concrete apron of the patio, which in turn steps over a low sea wall to the beach. The porch provides just enough protection and shade before the onslaught of the beach.*

FACING PAGE | *The long lines of the dividing fence make a nice counterpoint to the vertical composition of the bay on the north wall and the sweep of the waveform roof above.*

the footprint of the new house and patio almost filled it up, so the architect carefully controlled all the remaining exterior spaces and defined everything with fences and plantings. In the architect's words, the end result is a house that sits in a defined space "like a piece of furniture."

The Language of Waves

One of the house's distinguishing features is the waveform roof. This design grew out of the owners' request for a house that would be extremely resistant to wind, wind-driven rain, and salt spray. Techler felt that a curved roof would allow the wind to flow over the building more easily, would minimize uplift in strong winds, and would be a comfortable shape to clad in lead-coated copper, which was his material of choice for durability in this harsh waterfront environment.

At first glance, the curves are quite noticeable, but they soon seem a natural part of the landscape because the curved roofs are of a similar height and pitch as the surrounding buildings. The configuration of a long dormer with a flatter pitch is the dominant shape of most of the buildings along the shore, and the wave roof echoes this form. It speaks the same language.

BEATING THE WEATHER

One of the biggest challenges of building right on the water is dealing with wind-driven water. When it's windy, the air fills with spray and water flows uphill as if gravity didn't exist.

To keep the water out, the exteriors of waterfront houses need to be detailed almost as if they're going to be submerged. Flashing, which is the metal or fabric used to cover joints where

materials meet, needs to be sealed at edges, and any holes where the wind can drive in need to be eliminated.

A major cause of leaks is infiltration around windows and doors. Rain drives up under the flashing that in a traditional installation counts on gravity to drain water back out. The first line of defense is to get windows and doors with a high rating

against wind infiltration. The second is to install shallow pans under the windows and doors, so that if water is driven past the flashing it will just lie in the pan and then eventually drain back out to the outside rather than onto your Persian rug.

In the recent past, a major culprit for leaks was the vents in the roof soffit and ridge that were required for ventilating the

roof. With the development of new sprayed insulation, roof vents—and a major source of potential water infiltration—can be eliminated.

A Friendly Fence

One of the joys of living right on the beach is that you get to enjoy the feel of the sand between your toes. One of the drawbacks is that everyone else wants to enjoy it too. A public access path passes close by the house along the north side of the property, and countless beachgoers trudge back and forth throughout the summer. Tim wanted to give his clients privacy in their very limited outdoor space, but the owners didn't want to put up a high fence that would be an affront to passersby.

The compromise was to build a long fence of widely spaced horizontal boards along the public thoroughfare. The line between public and private is clear, and the owners feel protected, but the fence has enough transparency to allow filtered views in either direction. The horizontal line of the fence contrasts with a vertical bay on the north end, which lends visual interest to this side of the building.

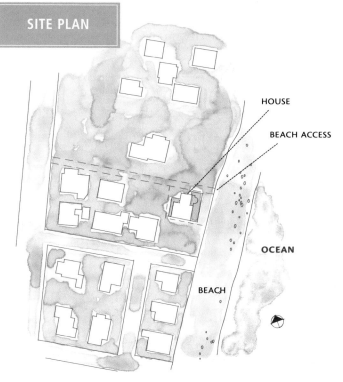

SITE PLAN

HOUSE

BEACH ACCESS

OCEAN

BEACH

ABOVE | *From the command center of the kitchen, the fireplace and the sitting area form a comfortable foreground with the beach as a backdrop. The simple materials, left in their natural state and carefully composed, give the interior a quiet sense of restrained elegance.*

FACING PAGE | *In an open-plan house, it's desirable to have a more intimate scale room where people can get away for some quiet time. As a bonus, this den has an attached screened porch, which is used as an alternative summertime eating place.*

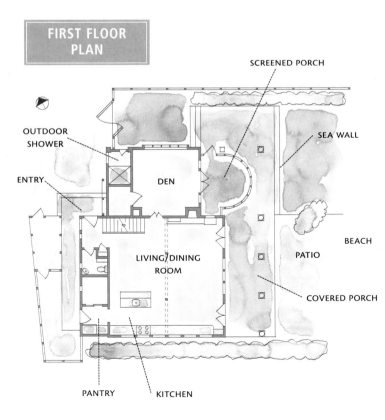

FIRST FLOOR PLAN

OUTDOOR SHOWER

SCREENED PORCH

SEA WALL

ENTRY

DEN

BEACH

PATIO

LIVING/DINING ROOM

COVERED PORCH

PANTRY

KITCHEN

On the Beach

Fitting into the rhythm of the neighborhood and overcoming the constraints of a tight site was the hard part. With the beach right outside the window, the easy part was providing a direct connection to the ocean. All the utility spaces, such as bathrooms and storage, are on the west-facing wall away from the water—what Techler describes as the "fat wall." We enter through this fat wall, and the living space spreads out in front of us, flowing through the French doors, out onto the covered porch, over the patio and the sea wall, onto the sand, and into the water.

The kitchen is tucked back in the southwest corner, handy to the pantry and the entry but in a position to look out over the whole living space to the water. The south wall of the kitchen extends toward the beach and then turns into a long window seat, which allows a seating place for non-cooks without intruding on the working space of the kitchen, which is very tight and efficient.

In open-plan houses like this one, it's a good idea to have an alternative living space where people can get away from the action. In this house, it's a den for TV watching or reading, which opens onto a curved screened porch that's used for waterfront dining in good weather.

The upstairs is just as directly oriented toward the beach. All the baths and storage rooms are on the west wall away from the water. Like the "fat wall" on the

SECOND FLOOR PLAN

PRIVATE DECK

MASTER BEDROOM

BEDROOM

BEDROOM

BEDROOM

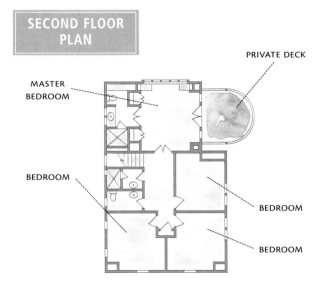

NOTEBOOK   WALL FINISH

Architect Tim Techler used an interesting technique for the interior wall finishes, which are tinted plaster topped with bowling alley wax. Techler mixes some of the tint in with the plaster right before it goes on the wall, which produces an occasional "flash" of color in the wall that gives it some life. The walls, along with the smooth finished concrete of the fireplace and the oiled Douglas fir trim, have a soft luster and wonderful feel under your hand.

The light line of the arched roof adds interest and focuses the view in an otherwise spare room.

ABOVE | *The line of the kitchen counter slides along the south wall, transforming into a window seat that's still within earshot of the chef. The wooden soffit above creates a mounting surface for the light fixtures and echoes the sunshade outside, making the scale of the seat more comfortable as it solves the lighting problem.*

BELOW | *The master bedroom and its balcony command the ocean view, and the bed and side bookcases are nicely tucked in under the springing arch.*

ground floor, these service spaces form an acoustic and psychological buffer between outside and in. The bedrooms are arranged across the eastern and southern edges of the building so they all have an ocean view. The master bedroom opens to a balcony carved out of the wave of the lower roof, and the line of the arched roof enlivens the bedrooms at each end as it springs across the building, providing a sheltering frame for the bed.

Going Barefoot

Even though the owners wanted an upgrade to a house that was a bit more luxurious, they were keen to preserve the casual feeling of being on the beach. Everywhere in this house the selection of materials and detailing reinforces that feeling.

Except for a couple of pieces of steel and the stair stringer, everything is unpainted and then either oiled, waxed, or left alone to weather. The floors are a dark Canberra, which is a relative of mahogany. Techler figured they would get "barefoot sanded" as people come and go from the beach, so he simply finished them with tung oil, which leaves a soft, matte glow. The floors can be re-oiled in the future as needed, with no worry about sand and scratches or dripping bathing suits.

LEFT | *Laser-cut steel allows this free-form stair to float in space, while the stainless-steel cable in the railing is so delicate that it almost disappears.*

BELOW | *The bathroom continues the use of natural materials with rubbed finishes that feel soft to the touch. Here, concrete that has been smoothed and waxed is used for a counter-top that is at once utilitarian and elegant.*

The minimalist stair with its zigzag stringer (the gray side piece) seems to defy gravity. It can hang in space like this because the stringer is cut with a laser out of a single piece of steel, which makes it strong enough to carry the entire stair with no intermediate supports. The effect is to create an austere, elegant sculpture along the side of the room. For all its modern accoutrements, this is still a house on the beach. With doors open in the summertime, there's a natural progression from inside out to the porch, onto the patio, over the seawall to the sand, and then back again. It's what living on the beach is all about. This house fits into the casual rhythm of the shoreline, with a modest added distinction, tipping its slightly more elegant hat to its older neighbors. ꙮ

A bedroom dormer is the only sign of the main house from the water, while the boathouse holds down the waterfront.

RESURRECTING A LAKESIDE BUNGALOW

THIS SUBURBAN HOME IN WISCONSIN is the second remodel of the original bunga-low on this steep lakeside site. The house had been renovated in a previous generation to conform to the real estate style then in vogue, which might best be described as "asphyxiated colonial." Sally and Kurt, the new owners, could see the bungalow-style house struggling to stay alive under the reno-vation, and they wanted it back—even though it would have to be reinvented from the clues left in the roof overhangs and the shapes of the dormers.

The owners consulted an architect first, but Sally couldn't see the house she wanted in the drawings he showed her. She turned instead to builders

The front entry, flanked by pergolas and tapered posts that are emblematic of the bungalow style, is a strong, well-ordered facade, in contrast to the rambling, more casual waterfront side of the house.

ABOVE | *Stretching across almost the whole lot, the house forms a barrier to the rest of the property, but the roof overhangs, pergolas, and porthole windows reach out to draw us inside.* BELOW | *The photo is of the house before the renovation.* [Before photo courtesy of Sally and Kurt Rivard]

FACING PAGE | *The sun porch wall is a symphony of windows, with thick wood mullions separating the large window lites and the delicate notes of the muntins framing the view down to the water.*

Philip and MaryVi White, whom she'd originally called in just to replace some windows. The need for more space allowed them to rethink the organization of the house, and the result of the creative collaboration between owners and builders is an un–self-conscious home that recaptures the Arts and Crafts spirit of the original building.

A Wall of House

Driving up the hill in this lakefront community, you pass by older, small homes and newer, predictable, larger ones, finally arriving at Sally and Kurt's house, which exudes personality without being ostentatious or cute.

Before the renovation, the house was an object sitting uncomfortably on a piece of ground; it didn't seem to belong. From the street, the new house is a shingled wall that runs almost the entire width of the lot, sharply drawing the line between the public space of the street and the private space of the waterfront side. It's an interesting wall, one that draws you in with its pergolas, tapered columns, tiny windows, and projecting entry. Because the wall is so opaque, there's an element of mystery and a strong desire to go inside and see what's behind it.

Inside Looking Out

Once inside the front door, a bank of large windows opens out to the lake on the western side of the house, instantly creating a strong connection with the water. From this vantage point, you realize that you're much higher above the water than it appears from the road, and the low sills on these big windows seem to bring the water right into the house. Surrounding the large fixed windows with smaller panes, or "lights," frames this important view, while preventing the window openings from looking like large holes punched through the walls.

MUNTINS, MULLIONS, AND LIGHTS

The vertical and horizontal pieces of wood (or metal) that divide windows into many panes are called muntins. These are the thinner dividers on the window shown here. Many people use the term "mullions" for muntins, but mullions are the heavier vertical pieces that separate multiple window sash within one larger opening in the wall. Because almost everybody knows what you mean when you say "window mullions," getting these two terms mixed up is no big deal.

The building industry generally uses the term "lights" instead of the more familiar "panes" to describe the pieces of glass in a window or door. So you will see descriptions of a "15-light door," which means a door with two vertical muntins and four horizontal muntins, which creates 15 individual panes of glass or 15 lights.

In the kitchen, rich cabinetry and dark colors are contrasted by the open space, vaulted ceiling, and big windows onto the lake. At right, a door leads to a side entry porch and steps down to the water.

Careful attention to details like this inlay in the sun porch floor gives a house a strong sense of composition. In this case, using wood inlays on the diagonal ties the floor back into the wood-floored living room and dining area.

In terms of their relationship to the water, there are strong similarities between this house and the house overlooking the Connecticut River (see pp. 184–191). In both houses, there's a sense that the water is right at your feet beyond the large windows. But whereas in the Connecticut house the long-distance view to the river was the dominant theme in a unified living space, in this house, each of the main living areas—sun porch, den, living room, and kitchen—deals a bit differently with the presence of the lake.

While the sun porch feels as though it's projected right into the view, a corner patio outside the den and the living room holds the lake at bay so that you feel more connected to that outdoor space than to the lake. The kitchen is focused inward, toward cooking and eating, but there's still a strong connection to the water through the large window beyond the granite eating bar.

Upstairs, the master bedroom has panoramic views of the lake, but the owners' favorite spot is the roof deck that they built between the master bedroom suite and the new garage (see the top photo on p. 59). Because the renovation called for adding a fireplace in the den below, Sally and Kurt decided to take advantage of the chimney run

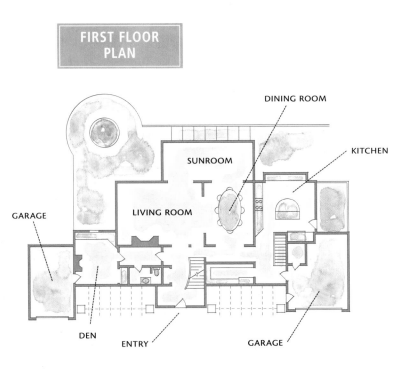

FIRST FLOOR PLAN

DINING ROOM

SUNROOM

KITCHEN

GARAGE

LIVING ROOM

DEN

ENTRY

GARAGE

LEFT | *The kitchen can afford to be open because there's a well-stocked pantry just a few steps away. The owners made good use of this space by building in a small computer desk at the open end of the pantry.*

BELOW | *The living room borders the den but has a much more outward-looking aspect. The detailing on the fireplace is echoed by the cabinetwork throughout the downstairs.*

Resurrecting a Lakeside Bungalow

RIGHT | *From problems come opportunities. The transition from the existing building to the new garage presented a thorny design challenge, which the builders resolved by adding a second-floor roof deck off the master bedroom suite. It's the perfect parents' hideaway.*

LEFT | *Bold use of colors gives each room a strong sense of individuality, but the sequence of three rooms in a row with rich saturated colors against natural and white painted trim makes the interior hang together.*

and add an outdoor fireplace here as well, creating a private, sheltered roof deck that's a secret "parent place" where they can chill out, contemplate the lake, and grab some time alone.

A Casual Sense of Order

While the street side of the house forms a formidable barrier, the waterside is much more transparent. A composition of separate rooms, each with its own roofline and wall of windows, the house wanders casually along the edge of the lake and is held together on the inside by creative detailing and the owner's excellent color sense.

The casual room organization translates into a series of recognizable but understated shapes on the exterior. Here, the order is sequential rather than one big idea. If this house were composed of big, bold shapes or one easily discernible form, the design could easily have overpowered the tight suburban lot.

The den is a much more interior space than the sun porch, with only a single round window to the outside. The window looks out onto a corner patio.

A cascade of roof planes frames the "outside mudroom" deck off the kitchen. In this corner, the stone base and large roof overhangs bring out the casual cottage feel of the house.

On the water side, the main house wanders along the ridge above the lake. Here, the more informal composition keeps the house from looming unpleasantly over the site.

SITE PLAN

LAKE

BOATHOUSE

MAIN HOUSE

DRIVEWAY

As you move through the house from the street to the water, the rooftop deck above the small boathouse is the final stop on the journey from formal to casual.

Outdoor living spaces (a tidy backdoor deck by the kitchen, a patio with a hot tub on the southwest corner) facing the water are placed off to the sides of the house so they don't interfere with the view. Instead of outdoor decks looming over the water, a cascade of levels drops down to the water from the back of the house. This design has a number of advantages: It puts the basement at walkout level, lets some sun in there, and keeps the house from appearing too tall on its steep site. Landscaped stairs lead from the lower patio down to the water and a small boathouse. The boathouse is topped by a roof deck, a perfect spot to enjoy the lazy days of summer. ✑

Slung between two side boxes, the central space with its waveform roof and corrugated copper siding has a great sense of motion, reinforcing this home's strong nautical flavor.

A HOUSE
OVER THE WATER

WHEN CALIFORNIA ARCHITECT MAX JACOBSON (of Jacobson Silverstein Winslow Architects) first looked at this site in the early 1990s, there were only a few other houses nearby. Today, it is part of a thriving waterfront community, and the house fits in seamlessly with the urban landscape where once it had stood alone. Formerly an industrial waterfront site, the development comprises two rows of "lots" set up along each side of a curving spit of land off San Francisco Bay. Zoning allows building over the water, and buying a lot here means getting 50 ft. of frontage on the road and 96 ft. out into the water. House frames rest on large concrete pilings driven deep into the bottom of the bay.

Inspired by the owner's love of sailing and the fluidity of the site, Jacobson designed a house that's a model of nautical efficiency. The signa-

Corner windows enhance the sense of immediacy to the water and allow great diagonal views through the house to the harbor.

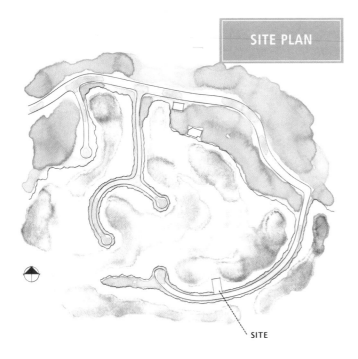

SITE

ture curve of the main roof sounds the nautical theme on the exterior, while the lack of wasted space inside reinforces the shiplike quality. Perched on about a tenth of an acre, the house solves the problem of getting as much function as possible out of a tiny site.

Boxes for the Land, a Curve for the Sea

Part of the challenge of building on this watery site was balancing the solidity of the land with the fluid motion of the sea. A long, low box on the west side anchors the house to the land and serves as a garage and sail storage area. To the east, a taller box stacks three floors of bedrooms and bathrooms under the 30-ft. height limit that's required by local zoning.

Slung between the two boxes is the main living space on the second floor. This space is enclosed by a curved roof and covered with corrugated copper siding. It's lighter and more expressive than the two flanking boxes, and the dynamic way it links the taller box and the lower box gives the whole building the sense of motion that the architect was looking for. Putting the main living space on the second floor also raises it above the bustle of the street and creates a portal to the harbor.

From the courtyard off the street, a waveform gate filters the view into the harbor and the private parts of this house. This is the only visual access to the house from the street. Once inside, visitors are greeted by a glass door on the east

A pen and ink rendering by the father of the current owner shows the house as it appeared before the rest of the street filled in. For a number of years, the house was the only building on this side of the narrow spit of land.

A false wall and pergola frame a sunny southern terrace, creating a transition zone from inside to out. Low parapet walls ensure privacy from the street below.

Viewed from the street, the long, low box to the left draws you into the site, while the vertical box to the right firmly establishes the solidity of the building. The reverse wave at the top of the gate echoes the wave-form roof above and opens to allow passage clear through to the water.

The stairway wraps around the second-floor living space and leads up to the master bedroom.

The open grilles of the painted steel stairs let the light through, making beautiful patterns in the stairwell and giving the sense that you are ascending to the bridge on a ship.

and the stairs to the second floor. Climbing this steel staircase flooded with light from above feels like climbing up to the bridge on a ship.

A Sense of Space

The stairway leads to the combined kitchen/dining/living room space on the second floor—and to the great view of the harbor beyond. The emphasis here is on elegant simplicity. For example, eliminating interior wood trim around windows and doors reduces visual clutter and makes the windows appear to float in the wall. The lack of trim also emphasizes the sense of the wall as a skin: It seems thinner and tauter, serving as a screen to keep out the wind and salt air.

In the main living space, the lift of the roof curve and the complementary curve of the balcony convey a wonderful sense of expansiveness. Picture this room with a sloped ceiling and a straight balcony and the effect is quite different. At the waterside edge of the room, the ceiling drops down to contain the kitchen, which includes a bill-paying spot with an uninterrupted view of the harbor (see the photo on p. 63).

The transition from the living area to the dining room/kitchen is marked by a curved line as

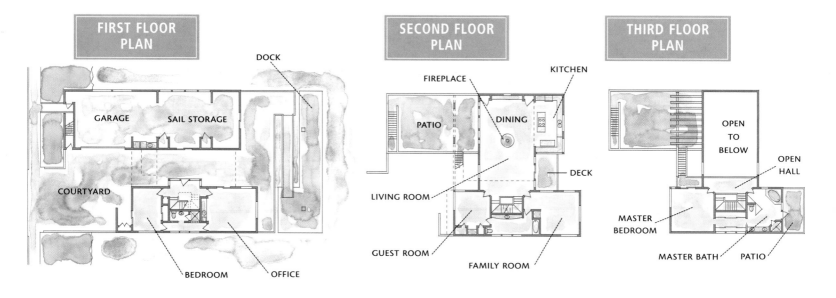

FIRST FLOOR PLAN

DOCK
GARAGE SAIL STORAGE
COURTYARD
BEDROOM OFFICE

SECOND FLOOR PLAN

FIREPLACE KITCHEN
PATIO DINING
DECK
LIVING ROOM
GUEST ROOM FAMILY ROOM

THIRD FLOOR PLAN

OPEN TO BELOW
OPEN HALL
MASTER BEDROOM
MASTER BATH PATIO

Eliminating interior trim around the industrial windows and doors reduces visual clutter and contributes to the feeling of refined simplicity. The wall is experienced as a taut skin that frames the view and keeps the elements out.

Viewed from the third-floor balcony, the carpet gives way to Chinese slate in a curving line. The rocks under the rotating fireplace emerge from the slate-like islands in the sea and serve the practical purpose of keeping people away from the hot fireplace.

the floor finish changes from carpet to Chinese slate. The slate continues out to the patio over the garage, creating a seamless transition to this outdoor living room. A pergola on the north end of the patio shades the dining room from the high summer sun and creates a transitional shady zone that encourages the owners to come out and enjoy this outdoor space (see p. 64).

Adding It All Up

On the interior, the curves, mix of materials, and varied ceiling heights combine with a restrained palette of colors and finishes to create a truly memorable living space. Here, the whole is more than the sum of its parts. On the exterior, the architect kept the house as simple as possible so there would be no distraction from the interplay of the boxy volumes and curved roof. The fine lines of the window muntins, the shadow lines of the board siding, and the vertical lines of the corrugated copper siding add a patina of refined delicacy over the basic form.

Being one of the first houses in a waterside development can be something of a mixed blessing. There's not so much

LOW-MAINTENANCE METALS

A "no-maintenance" house is hard to achieve in any environment, but it's doubly difficult by the water—especially salt water. However, using materials that naturally weather well in a waterfront environment can make a big difference. Here are some guidelines for low-maintenance metals.

Copper is the long-standing metal of choice for durability. It does well in saltwater environments and will naturally weather to a rich chocolate brown or, if "acid washed," to

the greenish patina associated with this material.

Lead-coated copper is the gold standard for weather-resistant exterior metals. It is pretty much impervious to weather. The natural silver-gray color remains largely unchanged, and its matte finish reduces reflectivity. The only downside, of course, is cost.

Galvanized metal is created when steel is electroplated with a zinc alloy that is highly weather resistant. It performs better in a

ABOVE | *From the master bedroom up on the third floor, the San Francisco skyline is visible across the bay. As on the main floor below, the absence of interior trim creates a very minimal look.*

LEFT | *Using glass block in the hall wall brings "borrowed" light into the shower stall without compromising privacy.*

need to fit in with neighboring houses, but there are also few local references to play off. This house succeeded in its goal of providing an intimate connection with the water and set the standard for the houses that followed. New houses continue to sprout up along this narrow spit of land, but this one is still the best boat in the harbor.

The lift of the roof curve and the complementary curve of the balcony give this room a wonderful sense of expansiveness, while the lowered ceiling at the room's edge defines the kitchen area.

freshwater environment than salt water, but can safely be used in both. It is best used for roofing and in structural applications such as steel columns, beams, and railing posts.

Cor-Ten steel is the trade name for U.S. Steel's "A-242 Modified" product. This steel gets a patina of rust—iron oxide—on the surface and then stops rusting. It doesn't work so well in a saltwater environment, but does in fresh water.

Stainless steel is generally a good material in marine environments, especially for fasten-

ers. This metal will always be shiny, so stainless-steel nailheads will stand out as a glittering row in the sun. It's also quite expensive. On the plus side, stainless steel is very strong and will outlast other metals.

Raw aluminum is not a great material to use in a saltwater environment unless it is protected with a painted or "anodized" finish. Aluminum is a good substrate for paint, so if the factory-applied paint is of good quality, it should wear well.

With twin gables, a full-length porch, rocking chairs, and beach roses, the house turns its summerhouse face to the water.

A HOUSE OF MANY FACES

SPENDING A LOT OF TIME ON A PIECE OF PROPERTY before deciding on a site will usually result in the right one getting chosen. Steven, the owner of this house on an island off the coast of Maine, had been coming here for 17 years before deciding to build. He'd camped in a small grove of trees with a view of the water, and he knew exactly where he wanted the house. When architect Roc Caivano came out to site the house with Steven and his wife Barbara, the fog was so thick you couldn't see the shore. But Steven was able to stand on the site and point directly at the invisible long-distance view because it was so clearly etched in his memory.

The house is on a large piece of property that has no shortage of dramatic sites, but, interestingly, the owner didn't choose to locate it on the most

A corner tower helps make the transition from the somewhat austere farmhouse facade on the landward side to the more expansive summerhouse overlooking the water.

Precise shadow lines on white clapboard walls, the silver-gray sheen of cedar shingles, twin gables, and a full-length porch reveal that this house's roots are in the vernacular 19th-century style.

commanding headland. Instead, the house is set back from the water in the middle of a field, balanced between land and sea. It doesn't command the site but instead is a quiet part of it, and you take it in with the woods, the water, and the field. It's just where a farmer might have set the house.

Split Personality

Approaching the house by land, you drive through the woods along a long winding road cleared just enough that you know someone lives close by. Cross over a dike between a marsh and a saltwater wetland and what looks like a classic 19th-century New England farmhouse comes into view. But if you wander around to the water side, the farmhouse is transformed into a relaxed Maine summerhouse, complete with full front porch, rocking chairs, and beach roses.

The architect could have chosen either one of these personalities for the entire house, but he felt that the water side deserved a more casual treatment than the more austere farmhouse facade that seems so natural on the approach. Though the house has two different faces, a relaxed familiarity punctuated with creative details pulls the design into a cohesive whole.

SITE PLAN

PINK SAND
BEACH

MEADOW

POPPLE STONE BEACH

SPRUCE WOODS

BAY

GRANITE LEDGES

From the wainscoting to the stair rail and the architect-designed light fixture, custom details, quietly suggested, make the design hang together.

The entry hall is distinguished from the rooms of the house by the green-painted wainscoting and trim, which conveys the sense that you've arrived in a "place" not just a passage.

White cabinets, linoleum on the floor, and rounded counter edges lend a touch of the 1950s to an otherwise contemporary kitchen.

A Screen Door that Slams

While it was Steven's intimate knowledge of the property that determined the site for the house, it was a casual comment from Barbara that helped shape the overall spirit. She told Caivano that she'd be happy if she had a house "with a screen door that slams," by which she meant a house like the one she'd grown up in—one that had "rooms" rather than "spaces" and that fit in with the tradition of the 19th-century houses that predominate on this island.

Entry to the house from the landward side is through a Dutch door, with a direct passage through to the water. The entry hall sets the tone for the house, with walls and doorways rather than wide open views. It's a house that encourages you to stop awhile rather than race through to the water.

The kitchen is equipped with modern appliances but because of subtle touches like the linoleum on the floor, the white painted woodwork, the rounded counter edge, and the wooden Venetian blinds, it feels as though it has one foot in the 1950s. This feeling is reinforced by the fact that the kitchen is actually a room, surrounded by four walls. It does have a wide opening to the dining room beyond, but there isn't the sense that the kitchen is an island in a "great room" as in many contemporary homes.

FIRST FLOOR PLAN

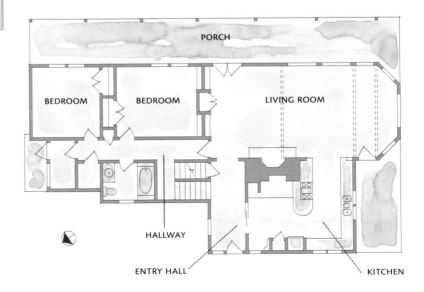

PORCH

BEDROOM   BEDROOM   LIVING ROOM

HALLWAY

ENTRY HALL   KITCHEN

ABOVE | *In the living room, a restrained color palette and simple trim form the backdrop for the owners' casual furniture. The emphasis is on comfort rather than style.*

LEFT | *Repeating cutouts in the stair railing reflect the owner's love of bird watching. Varying the profile of the cutouts slightly makes it appear that the birds are in motion.*

Old stones from a nearby foundation, with a few smoothed "popple" stones from the beach, frame an understated fireplace, which serves as a focal counterpoint to the big windows facing the ocean.

Casual Comfort

The living room is a little more expansive and has the air of an old farmhouse that's been modernized by taking down a wall or two. The room looks out to the water across the field, but it's not dominated by the view. It's as much about being inside as it is about panoramic views. Everything is quiet suggestion here rather than grand gesture. There's some comfortable furniture, but no sign of a decorator. Instead of a massive stone fireplace, there's a modest hearth made from three slabs of granite taken from an old foundation on the property. A few rounded "popple" stones from the beach connect the hearth to the site.

The master bedroom occupies the corner tower, providing a wraparound view from the water back onto the land.

An ample bathroom with minimal clutter takes advantage of the great view over the water.

While the design may seem casual and unplanned, a lot of what makes this house work is the result of the architect's careful detailing of paneling, bookcases, and trim. All the wainscoting is custom milled (instead of using available stock), allowing subtle changes of scale from room to room. Similarly, all the trim is sized to fit, which makes each room feel right individually and also as a part of the whole. In the interests of integrated design, Caivano even designed the light in the entry hall.

Upstairs, the pattern continues, with more discrete rooms and unassuming design. The master bathroom is almost as big as the master bedroom, calling to mind 19th-century homes where bathrooms were typically retrofitted by taking over a bedroom. These were rooms where there was plenty of space for bureaus and chairs and whatever other furnishings the owners desired. Another benefit of a big second-floor bathroom? Better views to the ocean beyond.

While many contemporary architects feel that it's necessary to make a statement when designing a traditional-style house, dressing it up with clever details that showcase their originality, architect Roc Caivano was happy to defer to the spirit of the 19th century. In his own words, he confesses to being "awed by the conventional." This farmhouse-cum-summerhouse proudly reveals its historical roots and, like an anchor on this remote island, pulls us inside and shelters us by connecting us to our collective past. ↶

NEW DETAILS FOR OLD HOUSES

For an architect, part of the challenge of creating a house that refers back to an earlier style is dealing with design situations that weren't an issue for an earlier generation of builders and designers.

Take vents, for example. Builders didn't need to incorporate vents in 19th-century houses because the buildings weren't insulated; moisture vapor and condensation weren't a problem because the wind more or less blew through cracks in the house. With improvements in insulation technology, however, some form of venting is essential in any conventionally insulated house.

On this island house, Roc Caivano incorporated an unobtrusive soffit vent that blends perfectly with the style of the house. The narrow vent strip parallels the roof edge, framing the soffit with a precise black line. Subtly decorative, it looks like it belongs on a 19th-century farmhouse.

The main waterfront porch has the rough and ready appearance of a wharfside warehouse.

The powerful, barnlike form of the main roof sweeps down to the lower-pitched roofs, which embrace the porches that extend over the water.

WHERE PORCH IS KING

PORCHES ARE THE GREAT INTERMEDIATE ZONES between being outside at the mercy of the elements and being inside and in control. On the porch, you're closer to the edges, shifting from inside to outside and often from land toward water.

In New England, where I live, the porch has an emblematic function as a reminder of a slower, more contemplative time. It also has practical uses as a buffer against bad weather and as a transition zone where you gradually shed the protection of the house. In the lowlands of South Carolina, where this house is located, the porch is a survival tool, providing pools of shade around the living space in the heat of the day.

The design team at Historical Concepts, the architectural firm for this retreat on a small tree-lined lake, had a very straightforward idea for the

The two-story space is made to feel more human scaled by running a wide shelf around the room above the openings to the porch. Without it, the room would seem cavernous.

Spot the antique. A new light fixture (at right) keeps good company with an older lamp (below).

house: Take the kind of large open space you'd find in a barn and enclose it with porches on all sides, each with a function that grows out of its location and relationship to the sun and the water. On the outside, the porches give the building a graceful sweep of roof from the 25-ft. peak down to the height of a person at the edges. On the inside, the porches add a perimeter of smaller-scale spaces that help to create a comfortable home.

Simple Entry, Simple Plan

The approach from the access road is low key, which is just what you'd expect as you drive up to a seemingly utilitarian farm building. A simple shed roof provides some shade at the south-facing entry porch, beyond which a set of sliding barn doors opens to the soaring interior. The floor plan is simple, with essentially one large room divided by columns and beams, and a bedroom, two baths, and a laundry room. With comfortable couches and assorted historic bric-a-brac, the feeling in the central space is of a renovated barn, a place for guests to kick back and have a good time.

Traditionally, high ceilings and fans kept houses cool in this part of the world. Now, most places are air-conditioned, but the design team wanted to

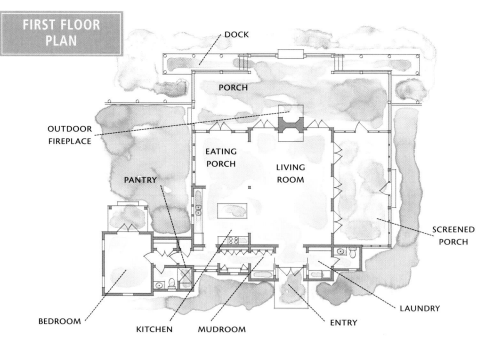

FIRST FLOOR PLAN

DOCK
PORCH
OUTDOOR FIREPLACE
EATING PORCH
LIVING ROOM
PANTRY
SCREENED PORCH
BEDROOM
KITCHEN
MUDROOM
ENTRY
LAUNDRY

ABOVE ┃ *The low porch over the entry changes the scale of the high barn wall, provides shelter from the rain and shade from the sun, and leads you inside to the main room. A mirror over the fireplace gives the impression that you can see right through the house.*

LEFT ┃ *Pools of shade under the porch roofs shield the house from the hot summer sun.*

With simple cabinets, a plain farmhouse table, and a bare minimum of appliances, the kitchen continues the barn aesthetic of the rest of the house.

retain the feel of the bygone era. So, although the house is air-conditioned, there are also ceiling fans and high windows that look like they open. It's a subtle trick, but when you're sitting here feeling cool and comfortable, you think it's because of the fans and the layout rather than the unobtrusive air conditioning.

Breaking Down the Scale

There's a danger that big two-story spaces can seem overwhelming. To avoid this, Historical Concepts broke the scale down by running a broad cornice molding all around the room just above door height. The molding divides the room into upper and lower halves. Green-painted trusses in the upper half further break down the scale and reinforce the barnlike quality of the space. A canoe stowed up in the rafters provides the finishing touch.

Detailing is simple and direct, as it would be in a fixed-up barn. Where new things need to mix with old, the design team has carefully updated rather than copied—as in the new version of an old light fixture. The newer one is simpler and a bit more elegant, but it doesn't feel like an overworked copy of the original. The two fixtures are comfortable together.

AT THE EDGE OF THE PORCH

For a porch at the water's edge, common sense (and code) dictates that you need something to prevent you from falling into the water. Providing protection around waterfront porches can be a challenge because, while you want something that contains you and makes you feel safe, you don't want something that blocks your view or corrals you like sheep in a pen.

On the waterfront porch featured here, the railing is so simple that it almost seems like an afterthought, but it solves the dilemma of containment versus transparency. And its down-home aesthetic is in keeping with the rest of the house.

Other solutions are to use a low wall topped with a rail to reach the required code height (typically 42 in.); stainless-steel

cables in combination with a rigid material; pipe and wood railings; or the traditional white wooden railing and fence. Iron railings can combine delicacy and a good deal of transparency with the strength to withstand the elements and meet necessary code requirements. You'll find examples of all of these throughout the book.

Dropping the ceiling down at the edge of the living room creates a more intimate space for dining in a glassed-in porch.

A Ring of Porches

The flanking porch on the west side of the building is actually part of the main space, but here the ceiling is lower, providing greater intimacy for inside dining and a sense of separation from the living area. A kitchen with a simple farmhouse worktable tucks in the corner behind the eating porch.

From the main space, six sets of French doors open onto the porches that wrap around the east and north sides of the house. The screened porch is primarily used for sleeping, but the main event is the waterfront porch, which spreads out across the lake front and creates a cool pool of shade on the north side of the living room. An outdoor fireplace provides a backdrop for twilight barbecues, while the low roof at the edge of the porch frames the view of the lake. Here you can flop in a rocker and watch the heron fish, enjoying the simple pleasures of a great waterfront porch. ꙅ

Sleeping quarters (complete with screened porch, of course) are in a small shed tacked onto the west end of the building.

With long views, no cars, and parklike promenades on both sides, the canals of Venice, California, are an idyllic urban setting in a public open space.

PRESERVING PRIVACY IN A PUBLIC PLACE

THE CANALS OF VENICE, CALIFORNIA, built by visionary developer Abbot Kinney in the early 1900s, are a unique setting for a waterside home. With parklike promenades on either side of the watery thoroughfare and not a car in sight, the neighborhood is idyllic but it still has an urban feel. Contained by the grid of canals, the neighborhood developed more densely than most southern California communities. The scale is small, everything seems closer together, and there's a richer fabric of urban life than we are accustomed to in many sprawling western United States cities.

The challenge with a house that's so close to the water and to the public walkways is to engage the house with the canal and garden while maintaining privacy inside.

ABOVE | *Because the space between the houses is so tight (only about 6 ft.), it feels as though you're already inside when standing at the entry garden. From the entry, you can look through the house to the canal beyond.*

BELOW | *The photo shows the view back toward the entry garden.*

Projecting the conversation area out into the garden breaks up the flat glass wall and increases the sense of shelter within the main living space. Here, there's an extra step up to the deck, and the built-in seat flows out into the living area.

A Graceful Entry

While the site conditions contribute to the appeal of this location, they also impose some design constraints. Because space is at a premium, the canal-front lots are long and narrow (90 ft. by 30 ft.), running from the canal to the service street behind. The first design challenge is getting people from the street into the water-focused living spaces in a graceful and efficient manner.

Rather than having people enter through the street-facing garage, architect Glen Irani created an entry path along the side of the house. The path leads down the north side of the house to a small entry garden that is almost hidden from the street. The sun reflecting off the south-facing stucco wall of the neighboring house creates a soft suffused glow, and the hustle and bustle of the street is quickly forgotten. It's a place to pause, then look through the main living space in the house and out to the brightness of the canal. Because the entry is away from the street, privacy isn't an issue here, and the architect was able to design a transparent entry wall that's an appealing invitation to go inside.

Balancing Public and Private

Although privacy isn't an issue at the entry side, it is a major concern on the side that overlooks the canal. The walking paths along both sides of the canal are just a few feet from the front of the building, which means that the house faces a very public space. The challenge was to bal-

The living room furniture, the dining table and chairs, and the conversation area beyond are islands of repose in the sea of concrete that flows from the entry to the garden.

FACING PAGE AND ABOVE | *The elevated "threshold deck" creates a definite boundary zone between inside and out, public and private, even with the large sliding wall in the open position.*

ance the desire for connection to the water against the need for privacy and security inside the house.

To take advantage of the view to the water, the wall facing the canal is almost all glass, but Irani has made some careful allowances so that the occupants feel secure enough to enjoy the connection to the public space of the canal. The lush landscaping of the waterside garden serves to filter the stares of curious passersby, but the most important architectural gesture is the raised platform that extends from a few feet outside the house to a couple of feet inside, creating a subtle barrier between the two. Called a "threshold deck" by architect Irani, this platform is one step up from the garden and runs the full width of the door opening. From the outside, the deck floats above the level of the garden and, even with the door open, creates a clear boundary to the inside of the house. From the inside, the raised deck increases the sense of being contained by the building.

To enhance the connection between the house and the garden, the custom glass door is a single large sliding panel that moves off to the side. When it is open, the door is parked alongside the building and any sense of "door" is gone—there is just the opening connecting you to the garden, but always with the threshold deck acting as a subtle barrier.

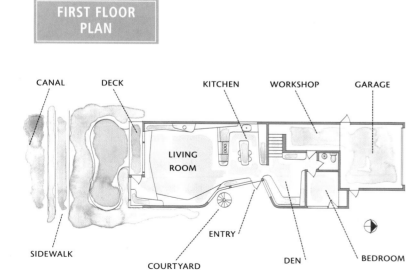

FIRST FLOOR PLAN

CANAL   DECK   KITCHEN   WORKSHOP   GARAGE

LIVING ROOM

SIDEWALK

ENTRY

COURTYARD   DEN   BEDROOM

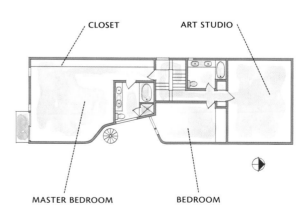

SECOND FLOOR PLAN

CLOSET   ART STUDIO

MASTER BEDROOM   BEDROOM

ABOVE AND BELOW | *When the design is stripped to the bare essentials, it's easy to appreciate the sensuous quality of the materials themselves. Here, the sinuous curve of the kitchen island counteracts what could otherwise be a cold abstract edge, while the fireplace wall in the main living space continues the sense of elegant simplicity.*

Adjacent to the large opening, the threshold deck extends inside to form a glassed-in conversation area. Projecting out into the garden, this is a different kind of transition space that allows you to enjoy the garden on the hottest days of the year from the comfort of the air-conditioned interior.

Smooth to the Touch

Throughout the house, the architect focuses on the essentials of design, with an emphasis on simple shapes and basic composition. But, at the same time, there's an awareness that the people living here need to feel comfortable. To that effect, Irani rounds the corners of countertops and other surfaces to soften hard edges and uses rich finishes to bring out the sensuous possibilities of wood and concrete. As you walk through the house, it's tough to resist the temptation to run your hands along the curves and smooth surfaces.

At the core of the house, a winding staircase is transformed into an ever-changing light sculpture. Because large windows here would only look at a neighboring wall a few feet away, small slit windows that let in intense patches of light are used instead. As the sun moves across the sky, small patches of light flow down through the open stair risers, creating a continuous light show that takes the place of an outside view.

Skillful manipulation of what is transparent and opaque sends messages to the occupants and visitors alike about what is private and what is public. The result is a well-crafted house that opens out to the water but still feels private enough to allow the owners to enjoy the public life of the canals. ∽

Light flooding in through small slit windows in the side wall filters through the open riser stair, creating an ever-changing light sculpture as the sun moves through the day.

A large master bedroom occupies the water side of the second floor. The trademark sliding wall panel opens out to a small balcony that projects over the living room bay below.

An outdoor terrace contained by dense plantings and a curved stone wall expands the living space of this small house on a quiet harbor on the Maine coast. The sense of containment makes the space more comfortable.

A SENSE OF SCALE

FROM THE WATER, it's hard to imagine that this house has only three rooms. Though less than 1,000 sq. ft., the house has a commanding presence, fitted into a site on the Maine coast that seems as though it was created just for this building. Starting with an existing shack on the property, architect Stephen Smith skillfully manipulated the scale of the new building so that it would seem to exactly fill the space allotted for it.

Smith realized early on that the key to making this tiny house big enough was to make the most of the available outdoor space. When you approach the house from the entry gate, you end up in an outdoor living room that's bounded by the house to the north, curved stone walls and garden to the south and west, and the water to the east. This patio space works

Glowing in the morning sun, the riprapped rock shore transforms into an organized stone wall under the house, and then dissolves back into natural disorder. The house's commanding presence is amplified by the compact site that the stone wall

ABOVE AND ABOVE RIGHT | *The entry walk leads down to the outdoor living room, while the small flared roof over the side door announces that this is where to enter the house. Because this is the street-facing side of the house, there are only three small windows, and they are staggered to bring light into the staircase and add interest to the facade.*

well as the living room primarily because it's on the south side of the house, where it's sunny most of the day. This spot is at the crossroads of the site—where you end up if you enter from the road, where you arrive if you have come to visit by water, and where you step outside from the inside living space.

Changing the Scale

Sitting outside on a terrace with a high wall at your back isn't always the most comfortable feeling because the scale of the house can feel overwhelming. Here, the architect has made this outdoor sitting space more inviting by introducing a break in the wall that changes the scale. A band of flared shingles and cove molding (sometimes called a "belt course") stacks the house into two layers like a cake. So now instead of a 16-ft.-high wall, we see two much more manageable 8-ft. pieces.

Scale is not size, but relative size. In this case, it's the scale of the wall relative to human size. A two-story-high wall is very big next to a person standing there, but one

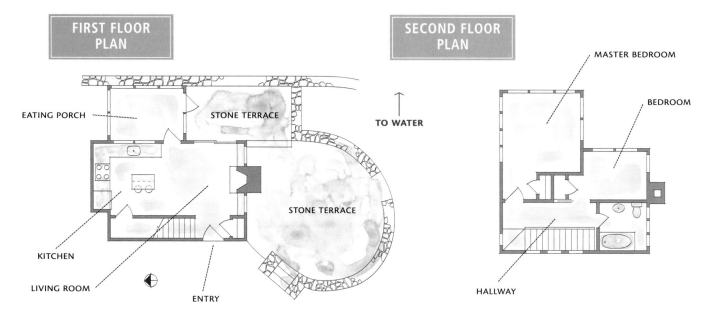

FIRST FLOOR PLAN

EATING PORCH

STONE TERRACE

KITCHEN

LIVING ROOM

ENTRY

STONE TERRACE

TO WATER

SECOND FLOOR PLAN

MASTER BEDROOM

BEDROOM

HALLWAY

The break in the siding at the second-floor line reduces the scale of the end wall, so the house doesn't loom over the diners on the outdoor terrace. Look carefully and you'll see the date of construction chiseled into one of the stones of the chimney.

that's just a bit taller than we can reach feels more comfortable because it relates to our size.

Moving around the corner to the path along the entry, the small flared roof changes the scale of the entry door. The roof provides minimal protection over the door and signals when you walk down the path from the entry gate that this is the entrance to the house. And when you go up to the door, the roof overhead makes the entry much more inviting.

Similarly, the four small square windows that wrap around the entry corner and step down the side of the building not only make the facade more interesting but also intensify the experience of walking down this narrow garden path.

GRANDFATHERED BUILDINGS

Existing buildings or lots are sometimes referred to as being "grandfathered." This means that the building or lot existed before the current zoning ordinance was written. Because the United States constitution prohibits the enactment of laws that penalize people after the fact, pieces of land and building locations that were legal on the enactment of an ordinance generally remain legal.

In Maine (and most other states) new houses cannot be built closer than the locally mandated shoreline setback, which is 75 ft. from saltwater in this town. But because there was an existing building on the site, it was okay for the house to remain close to the water.

However, there are often restrictions on enlarging or moving a grandfathered building. In Maine, you generally can't make the building any more than 30% bigger, and if you want to tear it down, the local planning board has the option of requiring you to make the building completely conforming.

In this case, there was no room on the site to make the building conforming, so the board allowed the owners to rebuild the entire structure because it was impractical to do otherwise—although they did request that it be moved back as much as possible (in the end, about 8 ft.).

A Commanding Presence

On the side of the house facing the water, the windows seem very large, almost intentionally "overscaled." In fact, it's not that the windows are huge but that the wall sections are small. Here, the manipulation of scale is not to create a "human scale" so much as to change the relationship of the windows to the wall. Because they are larger relative to the size of the wall, they make the house seem more intense and give it a stronger presence.

Another key to the power of this tiny house is the apparently small size of its site. It sits in a shallow niche that's carved out of the granite boulders that riprap the shore. As your eye moves along the shore, the random boulder pattern gives way to an organized stone wall that then flows back into a more random pattern beyond the house. The wall defines a space on the cliff face that's just a little bigger than the house—so the house feels bigger because it fits into this space that's "just big enough."

Just Enough

Inside the house, skillful changes of scale continue to make things seem a bit bigger than they really are. The living space downstairs is just big enough to allow room to

There's a strong sense of immediacy to the water in this upstairs master bedroom because the windows are set low in the wall. The "cottage" window style, with muntin bars in the top sash and a single pane in the bottom, allows an uninterrupted view to the water from the bed.

This is a small sitting area, but it feels just the right size for a number of reasons: The stones in the fireplace are not so huge that they overwhelm it; windows and doors lead the eye out to the view; and the heavy exposed beams in the ceiling are slightly overscaled, making the sitting space a bit more intimate.

In beautiful locations there is always a struggle between people who want to live there and people who already live there and don't want anything to change and alter their view. It has ever been thus, and planning boards and zoning rules are created to bring order to this eternal struggle. Just be sure that when you find your dream cottage nestled right on the water you make a few inquiries about the local zoning ordinances before you snap it up.

An alcove with a small bureau (in the guest bedroom) is an alternative to a closet where space is tight. The space above is for suitcase storage.

cook, eat, and relax around the fireplace, but there's essentially no circulation space in this room. To get from the front door out to the waterside deck, you walk directly through the sitting area—but that's okay here, because in a small house for only a couple of people, you're either sitting and talking or walking through, but not doing both at the same time.

The architect wanted to expose the floor beams overhead in the main living space, and he made them thicker than necessary from a structural standpoint. This also changes the scale, altering the relative size of the beams to the spaces in between and giving the ceiling a much more interesting sculptural character (as well as apparently greater height).

Low Windows, High Ceilings

Upstairs, two small bedrooms and a bath crouch under the hipped roof. In these rooms, the ceiling starts from a height of about 6 ft. at the outer wall and slopes up to the roof peak. This low eave height makes the rooms seem more cozy, but because the ceiling gets higher away from the wall the rooms don't feel claustrophobic. Using wide boards on the ceiling but painting them white and not exposing the joints makes it more interesting and reminiscent of old cottages.

NOTEBOOK   **DISAPPEARING WINDOWS**

In any house on the water, but especially one this small, it's important to provide a strong sense of connection between inside and outside. Architect Stephen Smith used a clever detail to do this in the wall between the kitchen and the summer eating porch. The window sash over the sink can slide down and disappear into the wall below, so the wall opens a view to the water and provides a handy pass-through to the porch. In the winter, when it's too cold to sit out on the porch, the windows slide back up into place, and the owners can pull up stools at the center island and eat in the kitchen looking out at the view.

In both the master bedroom and this smaller guest bedroom, the hipped roof compresses the space at the edge of the room and emphasizes the contrast with the view.

By setting the windows significantly lower than usual, the architect makes it easier to see down to the water. More important, the low window height makes the room seem bigger: Because we're so used to seeing rooms with window heads at about 6 ft. 8 in., if they get dropped a foot or so, we unconsciously make them higher in our mind, and the room appears bigger.

The same thing happens when very small windows get used, as in the bathroom and staircase. Here the tiny windows have a playful quality, but they also make the room seem a bit bigger.

Architects think about some of this consciously, but most scale manipulation is what any good designer does unconsciously when he or she is solving a problem. It's what we mean by having a good "eye." Good use of scale is often difficult to quantify, but in the case of this very small house the skillful manipulation of the relative size of things has played a big part in creating a delightful home. ⌒

A sweet curve on the vanity and three small sunny windows turn this modest room into a bathroom of distinction.

The homeowners' goal was to create a house that lives in harmony and partnership with the landscape. Looking like a fallen tree in the forest, the house is a perfect complement to the site.

THE ELEMENTS OF STYLE

FROM THE WATER, YOU'D HARDLY KNOW there was a house here, just a long stretched-out form that rises gently as it heads inland. It looks more like a fallen tree than a house. The owners are avid birdwatchers, and they wanted a house that lived lightly on the land—one that connected them to the immediate surroundings but did not overwhelm the delicate landscape.

To keep the house in scale with the site—a small peninsula jutting into a Montana lake—architect Peter Bohlin (of Bohlin Cywinski Jackson) made sure that the house stayed low to the ground so it wouldn't compete with the towering Ponderosa pines that surround it. The house stretches out from a rock ledge on the east to wetlands on the west. Instead of familiar house elements like windows inserted in walls, porches, and gable roofs, the architect

The warm glow of the interior is barely contained by the shifting planes of glass and wood that make up the walls and roof. Lit from inside, the insubstantial nature of this house as a solid object is readily apparent.

On the south side facing the lake, large planes of glass recede into the shadows cast by the roof overhang.

On the approach from the north, the house appears as a natural outgrowth of the landscape.

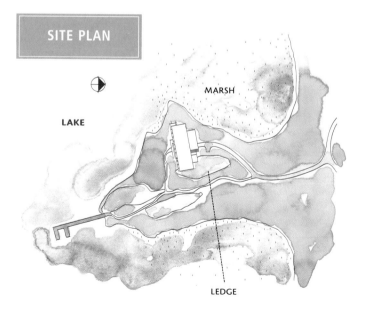

SITE PLAN

MARSH

LAKE

LEDGE

used a more elemental palette of planes of glass, wood, concrete, and steel, making us look beyond what we normally think of as "house."

Approach from the North

The entry to the house is through a cavelike opening on the north side, and here the elements of the house start to come alive. The stone patio seems like a continuation of the ledge next to it, rather than a manmade artifact. Walls and roofs aren't made up of the expected shingles or siding, but are planes of wood, steel, or glass. And they don't meet the way walls and roofs usually meet; the connections are more tenuous. Some walls seem to stop before they meet another, while other walls slide right on through. As a result, the house is experienced as a dynamic dance of surfaces, rather than as a static object.

The front door leads into the main living area, a big calm space with a roof far overhead that disappears in a latticework of beams. The room organization is clear and simple. There's a central wall, like a backbone, that slides through the entire house. To the north of this backbone wall are all the service spaces—laundry, mudroom, bathrooms, and mechanical spaces. To the south, the living spaces are spread out toward the lake, with the view screened through bushes left in place to protect the bird habitat.

Breaking Down the Corners

The two bedrooms occupy each of the southern corners. At one end of the house, the guest bedroom tucks in behind the living room fireplace. The floor here is raised a few feet as the house steps up onto the rock ledge under it, and the roof is correspondingly higher. Where the walls meet in the corner, a thin screen of glass and drywall gives way to glass and more solid concrete. There are so many passing planes

ABOVE | *The patio floor in the deeply recessed entry , seemingly a continuation of the rock ledge nearby, reinforces the illusion that the house is a natural outgrowth of the landscape.*

LEFT | *In the southeastern corner of the guest bedroom, intersecting walls and roof planes come together in the spatial equivalent of an Escher print.*

In the master bedroom, the lower ceiling height compresses the space, forcing the eye to follow the floor plane out onto the deck, which then dissolves in an almost invisible steel and cable railing system.

and beams sliding through them that it's hard to find the corner of the room. And because it's indefinite, it doesn't enclose us the same way a hard corner would. The roof plane is part of this visual trick as well, its beams sliding out beyond the glass screen to move us up and out into the landscape.

In the southwest corner, the beams and roof plane of the master bedroom are lower, and the space is more intimate. Here, the walls are almost all glass, and it's the floor plane rather than the roof that slides out, giving way to a deck as it crosses the threshold to the outside. Whereas in the guest bedroom the view is up and out; here the floor leads the eye lower, out toward the edge of the deck and the lake, where the railing of cables and galvanized steel uprights disappears into the greenery. In both these bedrooms, all the storage is built into cabinetry that feels like it's hung off the walls so the walls continue to act like screens or frames for glass rather than traditional walls.

By contrast with the dynamic wall planes and undefined corners of the bedrooms, the central living space is an oasis of calm. A concrete fireplace with an inglenook seat alongside forms the core of the house. Because it's two steps up from the rest of the living room, it has the feel of a dais from which the occupant can look out over the rest of the room. This is definitely the catbird seat, and in this house that's so in touch with the outside, it is a comfortable spot to curl up and be securely inside on a cold and blustery day.

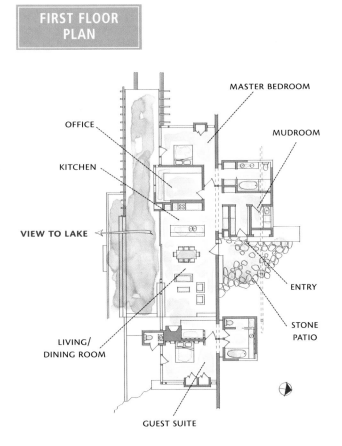

FIRST FLOOR PLAN

OFFICE

KITCHEN

VIEW TO LAKE

LIVING/ DINING ROOM

MASTER BEDROOM

MUDROOM

ENTRY

STONE PATIO

GUEST SUITE

In places, the exterior galvanized-steel surface of the central wall slides into the inside of the house, breaking down the barrier between inside and out.

A wall of glass on the south side of the house opens the main living area to the lake.
The kitchen at the far end is seamlessly integrated with the rest of the room.

An inglenook seat raised a few steps and a simple concrete fireplace form a core of solidity at the center of the house. The starkness of concrete, steel, glass, and natural wood is contrasted by the smooth, hand-friendly finish of all the surfaces and the rich textures of handcrafted textiles.

WHAT STYLE IS IT?

When it comes to house style, "contemporary style" is an interesting conundrum. Most architects think of themselves as contemporary designers—that is, they consider themselves "up to date." The public in general, and real estate agents in particular, use the term "contemporary" to designate a style of architecture that stresses compositions of flat planes and that has no historical references.

This style grew out of the Bauhaus design school founded in Germany in 1919. Its teachings came to prominence on this side of the Atlantic after World War II. Form was supposed to follow function, and thus reference to the history of architecture was considered contemptible, because this was the architecture of reason. In the hands of master architects like Ludwig Mies Van Der Rohe and Walter Gropius, some sublime buildings were created. Many of their followers, however, were less adept, and they gave us a generation of drab, repetitive boxes that most of the public quietly despised and certainly never considered living in.

In this Montana house, Peter Bohlin has taken Bauhaus principles and enriched

them with his own sensibility, talent, and sense of local building traditions—producing an indisputably contemporary style all his own.

LEFT | *Exposing the edges of all the materials reveals how the house fits together. Even the toilet paper holder figures into the scheme.*

BELOW | *With rock ledge just beyond the windowsill, the corner window seems barely able to separate the bathroom from the outside. The vanity top is a plane of stone, sitting on wooden beams that stick out of the front, mimicking the roof structure.*

Alive in Nature

All the materials in this house are in their natural state, and on the exterior they're left to age with the weather. The metal is either steel, galvanized with a silvery zinc coating so it will change only slowly, or copper, which weathers to a rich chocolate brown. The woods are naturally weather resistant western red cedar and ipe (from South America). Everything will slowly change according to its exposure to the sun and rain, developing a protective patina rather than requiring maintenance. As the years go by, the house will become ever more a creature of rock and forest.

The same materials are used on the interior, along with Douglas fir, but here they are smoothed and oiled to bring out their inherent richness in contrast to their weathered counterparts on the outside. In several places, interior walls are designed so we can see the supporting framing. Elegant glass and steel shelves are rabbetted into the studs to create a flexible display area.

Throughout the house, all the joints between surfaces are elegantly exposed and detailed so you can see how everything fits together. In most houses, trim is used to cover these joints, which allows some lack of precision. Here, with no trim, the level of workmanship has to be incredibly high. Even the toilet paper holder in the bathroom is integrated into the steel column in an elegant gesture that makes a bit of fun out of a fascination with details. ৩

Details like the double coursing of the shingles below the window sills, the flare of the shingles at the roof eaves and at the ground, and the wide roof overhang and the shadow it creates all serve to make the house seem more compact and grounded to the site.

Glimpsed through an opening in the trees, the house seems rooted in the bedrock of this Maine peninsula.

A ROOF
ON THE RIDGE

HOW WE APPROACH A HOUSE sets up a series of expectations that the house then has to deliver. This house by architect John Silverio on the end of a peninsula extending into Maine's Penobscot Bay uses a long, winding approach road to set the pace of the house. The road runs through woods, then down a long undulating meadow past clumps of old lilacs, until it finally comes to a copse of spruce trees with the peak of a roof just visible beyond.

The first impression from the land is of a welcoming entry and a series of roof shapes that cascade down from the peak of the roof. From the water, where the land falls away precipitously to the east, the same shapes come together in a compact set of interlocking forms fitted into the ridge that runs along the peninsula.

On the approach to the main entrance the stacked gable of the entry porch, the dormer window above, and the roof peak at top emphasize the strong sheltering form of the roof.

Well Grounded

Although the house sits on the spine of the ridge, you don't get the sense that it is precariously perched there, rather that it hovers above the ground. Silverio reinforced the connection of the house with the land by cutting into the ridge on the west side and bringing a driveway into the bottom of the house for wintertime entry. Here, the stone retaining walls reach out into the land, seeming to brace the house as it peers over the ridge at the easterly view. Keeping the land connection strong means that it's easy to move in and out of this house, and everywhere there are stairs and walks that create new ways to wander in and out and be on the land.

Cut into the hillside on the west, the stone retaining walls reach out into the land like fingers grabbing hold as the steep roofs cascade down to this lower level.

Walk One Way, Look the Other

Inside the house, the same sense of interlocking forms on the outside is echoed in spaces that fit together to form a larger whole without losing their individual identity. Movement through the interior is from north to south, following an imaginary line created by the ridge that the house sits on. It makes sense to lay out the rooms along the spine of the ridge so that all the public spaces get a view of the water to the east. And because the line of view is at right angles to movement through the house, it gives the house an added dimension and slows down our progress through

NOTEBOOK **DON'T BUILD ON THE HIGHEST SPOT**

Building on a ridge with a long-distance view, there's a temptation to go high. This is risky because you can end up with what one of my favorite architects calls a "cog house." Cog houses are those houses that you see everywhere that look like they were placed on top of a hill to engage the invisible bicycle chain that rotates the earth. If you are on a ridge, you don't really need to go higher—you're already there and the view won't get a lot better—but your house will get a lot more in everybody's view. John Silverio, the architect of this Maine house, was well aware of that and hunkered the building down, giving us its water views from the main floor.

Diagonal views from the living room in the center of the house sweep through to the dining room and the sunny kitchen beyond. The interplay of flat ceilings and rooms that are open to the roof creates a strong sense of compression and release as you move through the house.

the downstairs. The message is sit and stay awhile rather than rush on through.

Each of the major rooms has a view to the east, but they also look into each other to the north and the south. Some rooms have flat ceilings; others are open to the roof or look up into the second floor. And the second floor has a weaving studio (in addition to a guest bedroom) that spreads out under all the intersecting roof planes. This variety of space and view avoids a common problem of houses on dramatic sites where every room is focused on a single view: Once you've seen that view, the rest of the house can be a bit of a letdown.

A Sheltering Roof

Back on the outside, the shape of the roof and the large overhangs give the house a strong sense of shelter. A big part of this house's attraction is the way the entire roof system hovers over the house, an effect that's achieved by several design elements working together. The 45-degree roof pitch creates a right angle at the peak. When you look at the gable end (the triangular piece of wall between the roof slopes), this right triangle is a powerful and recognizable form.

Silverio emphasized the base of the right triangle by flaring out the shingles along the bottom edge, suggesting

PREVAILING WIND

FOOT PATH

DRIVEWAY

MAIN HOUSE

TEA HOUSE

BAY

STUDIO

that the whole roof system (including the gable ends) is a single entity rather than a bunch of disconnected pieces. The broad roof overhangs create deep shadows at the eaves as the sun moves around the house so the entire roof system seems to hover over the house like a low spreading branch on a tree, creating a great feeling of shelter.

Tucking the windows right up under the broad roof overhang intensifies this hovering feeling because they seem to be crouching under the roof. This also has the advantage of making the windows, which are really quite large, seem smaller from the outside because they are dwarfed by the roof form and are often partly or wholly in shadow.

The first floor of the house is composed of a number of linked individual spaces defined by framed openings and changes in ceiling height.

FIRST FLOOR PLAN

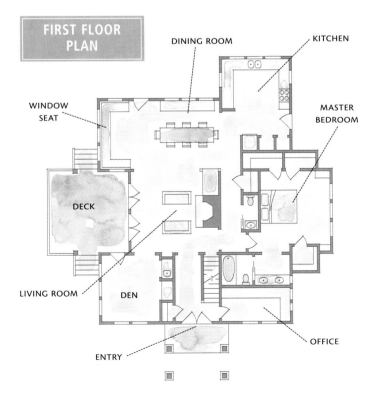

DINING ROOM

KITCHEN

WINDOW SEAT

MASTER BEDROOM

DECK

LIVING ROOM

DEN

OFFICE

ENTRY

ABOVE AND FACING PAGE | *The vaulted ceiling, elegant window composition, and tapered trim elevate a simple U-shaped kitchen from the mundane to the memorable. The side window affords a filtered view of the bay.*

LEFT | *The window seat at the end of the dining room is a casual counterpoint to the more formal eating space. Opening the room to the roof makes possible the drama of the higher window and the wide-open view to the water.*

Perched on the edge of the cliff below the main house, this "teahouse" was originally part of a much older estate on the site.

The wings of the house and a pergola above frame a sheltered deck just outside the living room.

The signature tapered trim detail continues in the master bathroom, helping to tie the design together.

Detailing that Works

Throughout the house, finish details add subtle continuity and another layer of delicacy. On the interior, the tapered vertical casing on the trim of the larger windows and the doors is the most noticeable detail. The head casing across the top has its ends cut in a complementary angle, completing the composition as it frames the window (or door).

On the exterior, a pattern in the shingle siding creates bands in the lower courses (rows) of shingles. This is an old trick that adds interest to the surface and seems to give the house a base, but it also changes the scale—the appearance of size—of the building. By creating a larger pattern, it makes the building seem smaller, and the sense of a base enhances the solidity of the house.

Good detailing like this is a recurring theme throughout the house, and, like a melody line in a musical piece, it quietly reinforces the uniqueness of the house as a composition. This is a modest house in terms of size, but its masterful composition lets it sit in comfortable counterpoint to the dramatic coastal landscape. ᴄ

Upstairs, a weaving studio spreads out below the sloping roofs and makes use of the low space under the eaves for storage.

ICE DAMS AND ROOF PITCH

Roofs are generally pretty steep in New England because they need to shed a good amount of snow and ice. It's the ice that's the problem. In the high mountains, roofs are often low pitched and built to hold the snow—because snow is an insulator. That tradition didn't work on the New England coast because with its many freeze-thaw cycles the snow melts and runs down the roof. When it hits the roof eave (the edge that overhangs beyond the wall), the roof surface is colder

and ice forms. It keeps building up and backs up under the shingles. This ice buildup is an "ice dam," which can cause catastrophic leaks. Steeper roofs minimize this problem because the water runs down the roof faster and is less likely to freeze and cling to the surface. With modern roof coverings, it is now possible to build flatter roofs, but steep roofs still feel at home to most New Englanders because they have always said "shelter."

The house forms a backdrop, creating an enclosed outdoor space on the lake. The screened porch is center stage in the two-story addition, which connects with the original building at left.

LIVING OUT ON THE LAKE

THIS SUMMER HOUSE IN NEW HAMPSHIRE started life as a cabin with glass on two sides perched on the edge of a lake. The family who summered here needed more space and wanted to live more intimately with the outdoors. Architect Dan Scully's solution was to create a building that allows them to spend most of their time outside by the lake.

As you come down the drive, the house initially appears as a long blue wall that blocks the view of the lake. But there's a significant chink in the wall—a gateway with a curved sidewall that sweeps you in, onto a deck, past the house, and out into the lake. It's a strong enough entry that you almost

The screen wall and door frame the lake, giving just enough sense of shelter without blocking the view. The decking material continues outside on the half-walls that flank the stairs, reinforcing the connection between indoors and out.

FIRST FLOOR PLAN

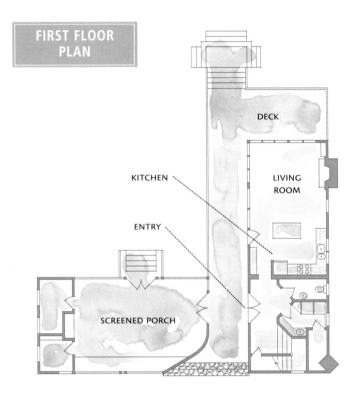

DECK

KITCHEN

LIVING ROOM

ENTRY

SCREENED PORCH

Looking back the other way, it's clear that the deck is the "highway" of this house, connecting screened porch, entry, kitchen, and lake.

expect to find handholds along the wall that you can grab onto to stop yourself from careering into the water.

Keeping What Works

Scully turned the entire existing cabin into a new living room and kitchen—right on the lake, with the best views. If this had been a new space, the architect might have been tempted to use larger lights of glass to capture the view, but salvaging the existing wall of windows gives this room a quality that would otherwise have been lost. The wall of awning windows has just the right balance of view versus enclosure so the room can be cozy at night but allow you to feel the presence of the lake in the daylight.

A Screened-Porch Addition

While the old cabin was transformed into cozy new living quarters, what makes this house special is the screened porch, which forms the base of one-half of the new addition. This is where the family spends most of their time now, living as close to the outside as they possibly can.

SECOND FLOOR PLAN

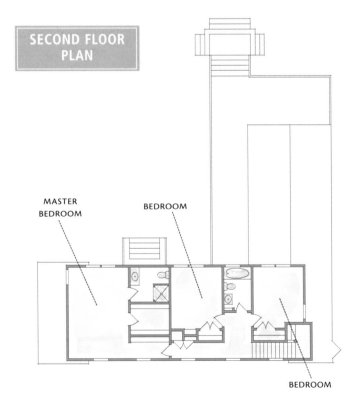

MASTER BEDROOM

BEDROOM

BEDROOM

The old cabin right next to the water is transformed into a cozy glass-enclosed room for use on cool days and nights. The change in wall materials at the entry to the room (left) marks the transition from the existing building to the new addition.

THE BEST ROOM IN THE HOUSE

Screened porches are largely an East Coast phenomenon. On the West Coast, there usually aren't enough bugs to make it worthwhile to screen a room. That's too bad, because a screened porch is a wonderful place, half inside and half outside, and when the weather's right, better than either.

The simplest kind of screened porch wall is a row of posts with screening nailed to them. This has the advantage of being relatively inexpensive, and it puts the least

amount of wood between the viewer and the view. It's a good idea to put a horizontal 4x4 at about 2 ft. 8 in. off the deck so people will know not to try and walk out through the screen. Also, adding screening under the deck joists keeps the bugs out at ground level.

The next step up in cost and complexity is building a porch with removable screen panels. The panels can be taken out in the winter so the view is unobstructed and/or replaced with similar panels with glass or plastic in the

frames. This gives more options for using the space, but it increases the cost substantially and puts more wood in the way of the view.

Some people like the convenience of being able to close off the screened panels at will. One option is to install a wall of sliding glass doors, but because the doors slide in front of each other you only get half the ventilating area. Hidden wall systems where the doors fold up like an accordion usually aren't screened, so if screens are needed in this sce-

Scully put a lot of thought into the design of the porch. Rather than screening both the lake- and land-facing sides, he made the landward (north) side a solid wall that curves into the entry deck. There is one screened area on this side, so people approaching the house can be seen and welcomed and the late afternoon sun can filter inside, but aside from that the room turns its back on the dark woods and focuses on the view of the lake.

Most of the exterior siding on the addition is "live-edged" wide board (made by leaving the bark on the sawn board) that is evocative of the camps along this New Hampshire lake. The strong, wavy, horizontal lines give a sense of motion. By contrast, the exterior and interior of the screened porch is a smooth, clear-finished cedar that's more restful and calls to mind the varnished cabin of a yacht.

Stock molding strips over rough cedar plywood mimic the exterior siding and create an elegant stair hall that's a radical departure from the original building and the more restful rooms upstairs.

Elegance on a Budget

The architect wanted the motion of the horizontal siding to continue inside the house, but he knew that using the wide irregular boards wouldn't work because the scale isn't delicate enough and the rough wood doesn't feel good to the touch. It's material that belongs on the outside.

To get a similar dynamic feeling inside, Scully used roughsawn cedar plywood and a series of stock molding strips. This combination re-creates, with much greater pre-

nario, you'll end up with a wall of windows with screens on them (this is sometimes called a "Florida room").

But a sunny room with lots of windows isn't that different from a living room—and you've lost that essential outdoor quality. My advice is to let your furniture get wet once in a while and forget about using the porch in the winter. When it gets cold and wet, go inside and light a fire.

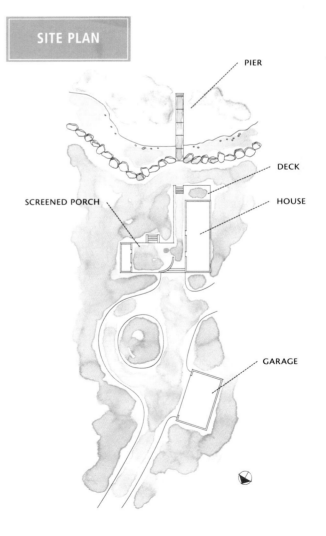

SITE PLAN

PIER

DECK

SCREENED PORCH

HOUSE

GARAGE

The horizontal lines of the exterior siding, but it's more elegant as befits the interior. Using the plywood and molding strips in the entry hall, which is the focal point of the house, Scully enlivens a small space with a sense of motion and dynamism. Upstairs, the strips and plywood turn a long corridor from a potentially dull passageway into a visual adventure. The wall is relatively inexpensive to install, because it can be done with large sheets of plywood that go up fast. And because the joints are hidden with molding strips, the result is a wonderful cross between cedar cabin and "Style Moderne" from the 1920s.

Simple and Compact

Inside the upstairs bedrooms, the walls change back to a smooth finish, without the horizontal banding. You've arrived, so there's no need for that sense of motion. Furthermore, what is neat in the hall would be busy in a space where you're trying to sleep.

The three bedrooms are basic and plain. In the master bedroom at the end of the hall, there is a desk built in under the eaves, but aside from that there is just enough space for the bed and a reading chair by the window. Looking closely, you can see there is a wide band of trim painted the same color as the wall that ties all the windows

The trapezoidal window in this small upstairs bedroom follows the angle of the roof trim, while the window trim extends out and around the room for an understated detail that subtly enlivens a plain room.

WHAT TO DO WITH THE GARAGE?

We don't usually associate garages with houses on the water. Clearly, they have stronger connections with the landward side of the house than with the water, and because the scale of a normal garage door dwarfs most of the portals of a house, architects generally try to hide them.

But this house is different. Architect Dan Scully has always had a fascination with cars and garages, and he designed this garage to be enjoyed as a sculptural object, in contrast to the more understated main house. The same live-edge siding used on the house forms the cap of the garage, but the lower shingled walls flare out. This provides some additional space down where it's needed without making the building overwhelmingly bulky. It makes it hunker down like a chicken ruffling out its feathers over a nest.

Instead of the standard roll-up garage doors, Scully installed an ingenious sliding

door system. The doors slide laterally past each another and bypass the passage door in the middle, which is outlined by two expressive vermillion painted columns.

together in an understated way, giving the room another subtle dimension.

Keeping all the indoor spaces relatively compact saves money because finished space is expensive. It also keeps you closer to the exterior walls and to the view. The smallest rooms in this house feel more like clothing than structure, and they make the larger screened porch seem positively palatial.

This isn't a house that's trying to make a statement with arresting shapes and ultramodern materials. It's about keeping things simple and focusing on what really counts—living outside in the screened porch and on the lake, which is what keeps this family here longer and longer every year.

ABOVE | *The curved corner at the entry helps to create a sense of motion toward the water, makes the entry more gracious, and at the same time gives the interior of the screened porch a distinctive corner.*

LEFT | *Upstairs, the combination of plywood and molding strips energizes the long corridor that connects the bedrooms.*

The brace at the end of the giant roof truss is engineered to resist the potential force of a mud-slide. It also nicely mimics the canted posts on the porch next door.

The house is broken down into two separate buildings—bunkhouse and main house—with a connecting breezeway between.

INDUSTRIAL STRENGTH

FOR OVER 50 YEARS, this secluded spot at the bottom of a cliff facing Puget Sound has been home to a cluster of unassuming cottages and cabins, known locally as "camps." Down here, at the edge of an otherwise predictable Seattle suburb, a small group of neighbors and friends have enjoyed salmon derbies, sunsets, and an incredible level of privacy with little change for two generations.

A few winters back, after some torrential rainstorms, the cliff subsided and the cabin that was here ended up in the Sound. The city was willing to let the owners rebuild, but only if the new house was constructed to withstand a similar event in the future.

Picking up on the rambling, down-home quality of the camps along this narrow strip of land, the rebuilt house fits right in.

The approach to the house from above is by way of a long wooden staircase that winds down to the beach. (Photo by Robert Knight)

SITE SECTION

That's when Seattle architect Tom Lenchek (of Balance Associates) got involved. Tom and his engineer, Jay Taylor, came up with a design that uses a series of giant trusses anchored into massive concrete retaining walls and the sea wall itself. The whole structure provides a frame built to withstand the horizontal pressure of a mudslide trying to push the house into the Sound as well as the weight of a pile of earth on the roof.

For added protection, Lenchek and Taylor created a built-up, laminated roof with alternating layers of plywood and insulation. Because these layers vary between rigid and ductile, like a Kevlar® bulletproof vest, the roof will withstand the puncturing pressure of trees, rocks, and other large objects falling on the house from the steep hillside above.

The engineering alone is impressive, but what really stands out is the way the building captures the casual rhythm of the surrounding houses and re-creates the feeling of immediacy to the water that gives these camps their unique character.

The southern facade is a physics lesson writ large in stone and wood, with concrete base, trusses, and braces ready to resist the forces that might try to push the house into the Sound.

Approach from Above

The only way down to the house is by way of a long wooden staircase that drops from the neat streets of suburbia down a junglelike cliff face to a small bench of land just above the beach. When the house was rebuilt, all the materials had to be brought in at low tide, when you could drive along the beach for a few hours. (You can still come and go this way, but you'd better know your tide tables.)

Approaching on foot from above, you come out at the south end of the house. Here, the engineering that drove the design of the house is readily apparent, graphically depicted by the massive concrete base, the lines of the roof truss, and the round column and brace that appear to be propping up the house, preventing it from slipping into the Sound.

Simple, inexpensive materials and finishes, industrial windows, and straightforward details ensure that the inside of the house is "beach friendly."

ABOVE | *The second-floor loft is hung from the bottom chords of the roof trusses. Galvanized-steel railings and the exposed stainless-steel chimney add to the industrial aesthetic of this beach house.*

FACING PAGE | *Dynamic trusses overhead contrast with the down-home quality of the interior finishes at living level.*

This south-facing facade is carefully composed with three large foursquare windows and a door. While the hand of the architect is evident in the composition of these elements, the rest of the house presents a much more casual face, in keeping with the vernacular houses along the shore. Casualness is a critical quality on this site because a house with too forceful an architectural presence would wreck the rumpled-shirt quality that has always been the essence of this community.

Beach Simple

Inside the house, the giant trusses define the space, creating a rhythmic progression that marches through the building. On a practical level, the trusses also provide the framework for the second floor, which is suspended from the bottom beams (or "chords") of the trusses. The complexity of the trusses creates visual excitement that contrasts with the intentional simplicity of the interior finishes. This is a beach house without pretense, where no one has to worry about taking off their shoes before stepping inside.

The rebuilt house is used primarily by the families of the two children of the original owners, and their wish list called for a main building with kitchen, living/dining room, one bedroom, and a loft above. The attached

WHAT STYLE IS IT?

Architect Tom Lenchek uses the term "beach warehouse style" to describe this unassuming house on Puget Sound. Part of the look derives from the heavy posts, or "peeler poles," which are the core that is left over after the outer layers of a large tree have been peeled away for plywood veneers. These posts are very strong, but they're essentially waste in the plywood industry, and here they get recycled. The ironwork for the truss is as the engineer designed it, with no attempt to disguise with fancy finishes. The windows are no-frills industrial sash, plain and simple.

While the design of the house was heavily influenced by the engineering demands of the site, Lenchek also took his cues for shape, materials, and detailing from the surrounding buildings. And, fortuitously, the steel braces that reinforce the roof echo the canted porch posts on the beach house next door.

RIGHT AND FACING PAGE |
*Steps lead down to the
beach at low tide from the
covered entry between the
bunkhouse and the main
house. A board laid over
the opening to the beach
allows uninterrupted
passage along the sea wall.*

*A corner window in the main space of the bunkhouse annex
looks out to the "notch" and Puget Sound beyond.*

bunkroom annex functions almost independently, though it
does have to share the kitchen in the main building. This
bunkroom annex turned out to be such a comfortable spot
that it became more than just a great place to sleep. In
fact, sleeping is relegated to a front room and the loft, and
the bigger bunkroom space is used as an alternate living
room. It's a bit more intimate in scale than the main building and trades the southern corner for a deck and a nice
corner view.

Breaking Down the Size

The two buildings that make up the house are connected
by a breezeway, with what the architect calls a "notch"
between them that functions as an entry court and a small,
private deck on the water. Stairs lead directly down to the
water (and to the beach at low tide), and a single plank
bridge spans the opening in the sea wall, providing a pre-

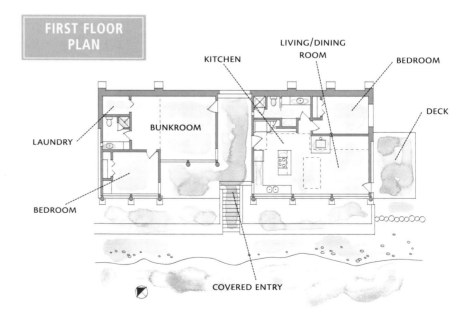

FIRST FLOOR
PLAN

LIVING/DINING
ROOM

KITCHEN

BEDROOM

DECK

LAUNDRY

BUNKROOM

BEDROOM

COVERED ENTRY

BELOW | *A bedroom on the first floor of the bunkhouse makes it feel as though you're sleeping right on the beach, while the deep overhang provides shade from late afternoon sun.*

carious perch for anyone who wants to stand out over the water at high tide.

Building the house in two parts with this connecting "notch" between gave the architect a chance to break down the size and bring it into scale with the neighboring houses' more rambling demeanor. The owners got to come back to a house that has a great deal of visual (and physical) strength, but they didn't have to give up the casual life they'd enjoyed in the cabin that stood here before. The new house fits right back into the neighborhood, and you can still leave from here for the salmon derby. ∽

Hovering over the water as if it has just slid into a boat slip, the boathouse stands in regal contrast to the dark evergreens behind it.

STANDING ALONE

HOW WELL A HOUSE FITS into the landscape is the most important factor in determining the success of a waterfront home. Some houses fit in so seamlessly you scarcely know they're there. Others make a bolder statement and fit in by being part of a strong composition. Such is the case with this boathouse on Muskoka Lake in Ontario, Canada.

A boathouse is a garage for boats, so it is actually built out over the water. Projecting into the lake, with a hillside of dark evergreens behind it, this building will always stand out and be seen as an object. So instead of trying to blend it in, architects Brigitte Shim and Howard Sutcliffe concentrated on designing a building that is a beautiful composition, able to stand alone with nature as a dramatic backdrop.

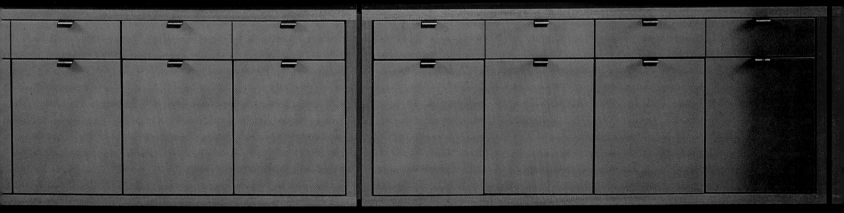

No mere service space, the bathroom is lavished with the same attention to finely crafted detail as the rest of the boathouse. And the views are without parallel.

The low wall on the upstairs deck provides just enough privacy from the deck below. An elegant rail at elbow-leaning height keeps you from falling over the edge but doesn't block the view of the lake.

Approaches by Water and by Land

As you approach from the water, there's an intriguing sense of roofs, walls, and exterior spaces sliding past one another, a little like a Chinese puzzle. Large roof overhangs that create dramatic shadows, contrasting natural wood and painted surfaces, and covered porches and open decks fit together in a rhythmic dance. The living quarters hover quietly over the boat garage, sitting regally on the edge of the lake.

The approach from the land is equally compelling, but as you get closer, parts of the building—roof overhangs, parapet walls, individual spaces like the second floor deck—begin to come into focus rather than the whole composition that is so successful from the water. From the lower deck, which is used as a family gathering spot for waterfront activities, an outside staircase leads up to a

A moss garden at the top of the entry stair conceals a flat roof and provides a visual connection to the landscape below.

"guest house." But the "guests" here are the owners; this is their retreat from their guests, who stay in the bigger house up the hill.

At the top of the stairs, a small rooftop garden visually connects the living quarters with the natural surroundings below. A stone path leads through the garden to the upstairs deck, which provides both a private sunspace for the owners

BUILDING ON THE WATER

Building a house at the water's edge is challenging enough, but when you build out *over* the water a whole new set of issues comes into play. For simple frame buildings where the soil is suitable, wooden pilings can be driven down into the mud to support the house. A heavier-duty version might use a framework of glue-laminated beams resting on concrete pilings.

At Muskoka Lake, where this boathouse is located, there's a granite ledge not far below the lake bottom, so driving down pilings wouldn't work. Here, a fascinating method of building "cribs" (wooden cages) filled with rocks was used. According to the architects, "It begins with the overall dock layout on the frozen lake during the winter prior to the construction season. The position

of each crib is drawn and a hole is cut into the ice, whereupon sleepers (horizontal beams) are laid to span and provide support for the entire crib assembly. As each crib is completed, the ends of the sleepers are cut, and the cribs are lowered

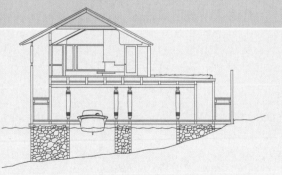

through the holes to settle on the lakebed. Before the holes in the ice freeze over, granite rocks are dropped into the cribs as ballast."

From the land side, walls, roof overhangs, and the space formed by the roof over the upper deck form a striking composition. With the door to the boat slip slid open, you can see clear through the house to the lake.

RIGHT | *From the entry, receding planes of wood paneling and trim, like layers on an ornate picture frame, focus the view on a window looking directly out to the lake.*

BELOW | *The kitchen occupies the passage between the bedroom and the bathing area. Here, corners and sight lines rather than doors define the boundaries of spaces. The freestanding wall at the edge of the hall gives some bedroom privacy but still allows acoustic connection to the small kitchen.*

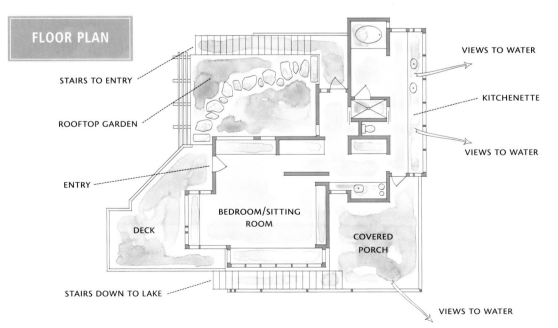

FLOOR PLAN

STAIRS TO ENTRY

ROOFTOP GARDEN

ENTRY

DECK

STAIRS DOWN TO LAKE

VIEWS TO WATER

KITCHENETTE

VIEWS TO WATER

BEDROOM/SITTING ROOM

COVERED PORCH

VIEWS TO WATER

and shade for the dockside deck below. The wall around this upstairs deck is set high enough to provide privacy from below, but low enough that anyone sitting there doesn't feel cut off from the lake. A simple rail at elbow-leaning height ensures that no one falls over the edge.

A Private World

Up on the living level, the layout is very simple, with just a bedroom/sitting room, a small kitchen, and a bathing area. There are no doors to go through up here (except for one in the bathroom) because this is all the private space of the owners. Separation is provided instead by distance and by turning corners. This gives the sense of being in contact with everything, but allows for comfortably sized domestic spaces and just enough privacy. For example, looking down from the kitchen toward the bed/sitting room a dividing wall is set to maintain the privacy of that space, but there is still a sense of connection through the narrow opening between the walls (see the left photo on the facing page).

In the bed/sitting room, mahogany-framed windows reach up to the curved wood ceiling, framing beautiful views of the lake. The curve of the ceiling adds a sense of containment, giving just the right balance of exposure to the view and sheltered coziness. This is a room that will keep you cool on a sultry summer day with all the windows open, but provide shelter and warmth on chilly winter nights with the fire blazing in the hearth. Wood is used extensively throughout the boathouse because wood finishes are much more tolerant of movement than drywall or plaster—and the architects knew there would be some movement because of the construction method used (see the sidebar on p. 134). The ceiling is a narrow-board Douglas fir, which folds down easily over the lakeside wall.

ABOVE AND BELOW *The downward swoop of the curved wood ceiling gives the bedroom the feel of a stateroom on a yacht. The lower height changes the scale of the space, making it cozy as well as beautiful.*

A peaceful composition and a breathtaking view conspire to make washing at the sink a memorable experience.

DELIGHTFUL DETAILS

There's a level of attention to detail throughout this building that belies its status as a lowly boathouse. Starting at the entry stair, a handrail that looks like a well-worn oar reaches out to be grabbed, the first of many carefully designed and executed details that give this house such a unique signature.

Inside, graceful custom-designed door handles fit perfectly in the hand, but they almost go unnoticed because this level of design is everywhere . Out on the deck, a light fixture that has to withstand water, wind, and ice is turned into an object of beauty that transcends the functional requirements behind its design. Yet you almost don't notice it because the patterns of light and shadow created by opening up the porch roof to let light into the bathroom provide a further layer of delightful detail overhead.

The green panel that appears to be sliding out of the wall blocks just enough of the window to give some privacy in the bed area.

Most of the cabinetwork is mahogany with a rich rubbed finish. An occasional splash of green in a cabinet front sets off the dark wood and brings out the mahogany's richness. The whole effect is reminiscent of a cabin in a yacht, combining rich finish and functionality and framing great views over the water while still giving a sense of enclosure.

The Art of Bathing

In many houses, bathrooms are little more than service spaces that take up only the least amount of the least desirable space in the house. Here, the bathing area is a celebration. Facing out over the lake, the quiet composition of bathing bowl, soft smooth wood underfoot and at hand, and a view framed by carefully sized windows all conspire to say, "Slow down and enjoy being here." At the far end of the bathroom, the bathing area has a wood-enclosed whirlpool bath with a slit window that allows yet another view out to the lake, the final flourish in a memorable lakeside home. ↩

Like a bathing area on a boat, the tub is surrounded with wood and the floor is mahogany duck board grating, which lets water drop through to the drain. A slit window at the head of the tub lets in a narrow slice of the lake view.

Seen from the water, the small guest house echoes the bolder gables of the main house, which peers out of the trees farther up the hill.

The waterfront side of the house puts on a very public face, with welcoming porches and bay windows.

A QUESTION OF BALANCE

ISLAND SITES ARE ALWAYS A LITTLE DIFFERENT from those on the mainland because the boundaries of island communities are clearer. When the site is "in town," as it is on this small coastal island in Maine, there's a strong obligation to use a design language the residents of the town are comfortable with. This doesn't necessarily mean that a new house built here should be a straight copy of the existing houses (in this case, predominantly 19th-century farmhouses), but it should respect its surroundings in terms of scale, treatment of materials, relationship to the street, and appearance from the water. Otherwise, it will never shake off the label of "that new place down the road."

ABOVE | *From the road, the house settles into the site like a first cousin of the Shingle-style library next door. The front porch welcomes visitors to the house, while its pool of shadow quietly preserves the privacy of the people inside.*

FACING PAGE | *Hanging out over the dock, the guest house is fully engaged with the water. Bright colors and informal furnishings are in keeping with casual beach style, in contrast to the more traditional look of the main house.*

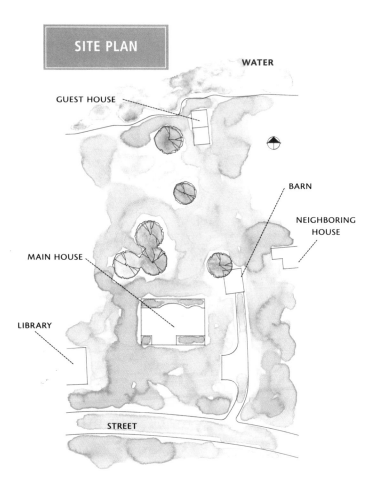

SITE PLAN

WATER

GUEST HOUSE

BARN

NEIGHBORING HOUSE

MAIN HOUSE

LIBRARY

STREET

Fitting In with the Town

The property that this house sits on features a beautiful old apple orchard that falls away to the west and northwest with a spectacular view over the bay. It came with a run-down fisherman's shack on the shore, which local zoning allowed our firm (Knight Associates) to rebuild as a very small guesthouse right on the water next to the dock.

Our clients, George and Patricia (and their daughter Sachi), wanted their house to strike a balance between the town and the water. To that end, they decided not to turn their backs on the community and build the main house right down by the water. Besides, the guesthouse hanging out over the bay would more than satisfy their waterfront needs. With that decision made, the main house could be put just where it belonged—in the upper end of the orchard where there was a natural space created between an old barn, some large trees, and the thinning out of the orchard.

The house nestles in between a Shingle-style library on one side and a white clapboard farmhouse on the other. Most of the houses along this road are relatively small, traditional, one-and-a-half-story, gable-roofed farmhouses, but George and Patricia wanted a house with a more open floor plan with a combined living/dining/cooking space. A large integrated space like this would be an uncomfortable fit in a 19th-century farmhouse composed of many smaller rooms. Instead, we designed a house with the low spreading roofs and porches that are a hallmark of the Shingle style. As a result, the house fits in comfortably

Large windows light the upper stair hall and staircase in this buffer zone between the road and the owners' private quarters. An interior window on the inner wall allows morning light to filter through to the master bedroom.

ABOVE | *The fieldstone fireplace serves as the focal point of the living room and as a divider between the private first-floor bedrooms and the public living space.*

RIGHT | *In an open-plan room without interior walls, it's important to provide some sense of separation between different functions. Here, the fir ceiling defines the dining area as a separate activity zone from the living area beyond.*

with the library next door and settles down nicely in the
orchard as though it has been there for years.

Looking In

One of the big challenges with any house is making it feel
welcoming from the street without compromising the privacy of the people inside. George and Patricia wanted their
house to be a part of the town but, at the same time, not
get the feeling that the town was watching. By recessing an
entry porch under the big gable on the east side facing the
street, we were able to create a space that's welcoming but
also in shadow for most of the day, making it hard to see
through. The shadow disguises the fact that there are few
ground-floor windows on this side of the house. So while
the porch welcomes, it also protects and conceals the
people inside.

With few first-floor windows, it was important to have
a large bank of windows on the second floor to get morning sun into this side of the house. But, again, privacy was
an issue, so the windows open onto a staircase and an
upstairs hall rather than onto a room. By day, light spills
down the stair to the first floor. At night, the lit-up windows present a warm glow to the street, but the private
areas within are screened from view.

*Although still part of the main living space, the kitchen area itself is sepa-
rated from the eating area by the big worktable and the field of hanging
lights. Douglas fir floors, cherry cabinets, and black Fireslate® counters
continue the warm hues of the stone fireplace in the living room.*

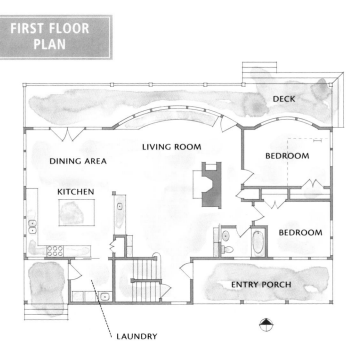

FIRST FLOOR PLAN

DECK

LIVING ROOM

DINING AREA

BEDROOM

KITCHEN

BEDROOM

ENTRY PORCH

LAUNDRY

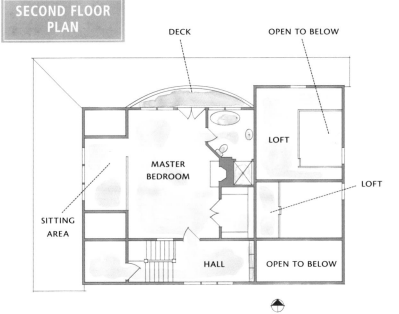

SECOND FLOOR PLAN

DECK

OPEN TO BELOW

LOFT

MASTER BEDROOM

LOFT

SITTING AREA

HALL

OPEN TO BELOW

One Big Room

The downstairs living quarters is essentially one big room. The challenge with an open space like this is to integrate different areas and keep people visually connected while at the same time giving each area enough individuality so that there's a sense of functional separation within the larger room. That way, one person can be reading by the fire, another cooking in the kitchen, and a third working at the dining table—all separate, yet together. A large fieldstone fireplace anchors the sitting space and is the primary focus for the people who gather here. Off to the side, a fir ceiling with a sloped edge, a field of hanging lights, and a large farmhouse worktable define the edge of the kitchen. A curved window seat in the bay creates another spot to hang out in, with enough room in front to allow comfortable passage to the door down to the water.

FACING PAGE AND ABOVE | *With its own small curved bay and window seat, the waterside bedroom on the first floor echoes the design of the living room, while the private loft sets it apart as a room of its own. The round window frames a view over the guest house to the bay beyond.*

Private Views

All the downstairs rooms feed into this main living area, but bedrooms and bathrooms benefit from a little more privacy, so the fireplace creates a small hall behind it that gives these rooms that sense of separation. On the water side, Sachi's bedroom is a miniature version of the house,

TWO-FACED HOUSES

On any waterfront home, there's a basic dilemma: Which side is the front? Realistically, most people will approach the house from the land, so it's important that the street side of the house be welcoming. But the house will still be seen from the water, so there's an obligation to make the side facing the water equally memorable.

On an island site, the waterfront approach becomes even more important, especially if the house has a dock. Depending on the tide and the weather, the owners of this Maine house come and go regularly from their own dock—and they often bring guests with them as well.

This means thinking about the water-facing side of the house in terms of people approaching the house. It's important that it not look like the "back" of the house, with no public gestures. In this case, the big gable dormers are emblematic of the house when you approach from the water. As you get closer coming up the hill, the porch, the curved balcony above it, and the curved bay windows start to actively involve you with the house and let you know that this is the real front of the home.

ABOVE AND BELOW | *The window seat along the curved bay leads gracefully to the door to the water. A hinged top in the window seat allows storage for the stuff that's used only once in a while.*

with its own small bay window, a dormer with a loft, and a round window that echoes the window on the main gable.

Upstairs, George and Patricia's bedroom and bath occupy the whole second floor and have the best views of the water, in contrast to the downstairs rooms that get only a glimpse of the bay. Having a first floor that is not as focused on a water view is in step with the 19th-century houses around here. Back then, the men worked on the water all day and wanted to come home to shelter—and this is still true for many of the islanders today. They probably want to be able to see their boat on its mooring, but aside from that, their houses are more focused on the land.

George and Patricia are avid sailors, and it's that connection that brought them to the island in the first place. With a dock and boats and a little guesthouse right on the water, the main house can be more about the pleasures of the land. In this community, that seems about right. ◡

RIGHT | *An old-fashioned tub, white wainscoting and trim, and modest fixtures are in keeping with the simple farmhouse aesthetic.*

BELOW | *The upstairs bedroom has a balcony outside, the best views of the water, and a small, simple fireplace for chilly fall mornings.*

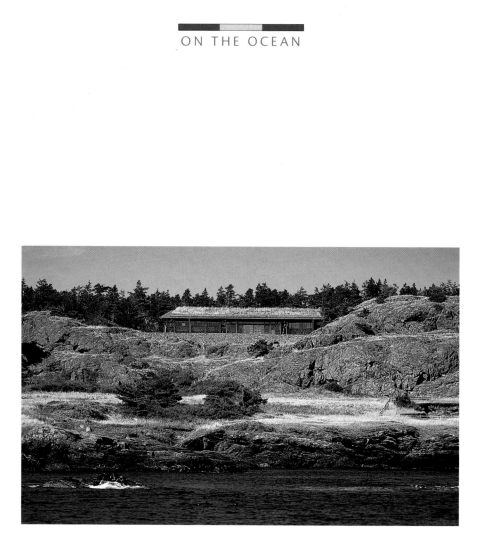

Appearing as a line of glass sandwiched between a slope of sod roof and a stone wall that merges with the cliff, the house doesn't call attention to itself from the water.

GRACE NOTES

TOM AND SALLY WERE SO ATTACHED TO THE RUGGED BEAUTY of this piece of property in Washington's San Juan Islands that they weren't sure they could bring themselves to build on it. They loved the high cliffs overlooking the Strait of Juan de Fuca and the Olympic Mountains but were afraid that a house might upset the natural balance of the landscape. Seattle architect Jim Cutler (of Cutler Anderson Architects) was able to allay their fears, and he designed them a house that fits in so well that it's hard to imagine the shoreline without it.

To sit comfortably in this bold landscape, the shape of the house needed to be bold as well—but not so bold that it would overpower the land. Cutler

The sheltering warmth of an inward-looking sitting area contrasts with the expansiveness of the waterside exposure.

resolved this dilemma by siting the long, low, narrow house in a notch in a cliff at the spot where the forest becomes a field and the cliff drops down to the sea. With its massive sheltering sod roof, the house looks like a natural outgrowth of the rocky shore.

Tom and Sally weren't looking for a house that makes a statement. Their wish list was essentially for a cabin, with a combined living space and rooms for sleeping and bathing. Cutler gave them three separate cabins set at slightly different angles and connected by the sod roof overhead. The parents' bed and bath are in one cabin, a dormitory wing is in another, with a communal living space in the center. The passages between the three units are also the primary connections back into the land and down to the water.

Forest, Wall, Mountains, and Sea

The approach road wanders through a quiet forest of old Douglas fir and madrona trees. As you get close to the house, the open sky becomes visible through the trees and there's a strong sense that something is about to burst into view. But what comes into view as the narrow road ends initially appears to be an impenetrable wall of house—until you see the two narrow passages that cut through the house and frame views of the water and the Olympic Mountains beyond.

A fundamental part of the experience of passing through either gap in the wall is the feeling that you can just keep on going, walking through the house to the terrace, down the stone steps to the field, and to the water beyond. The initial impression is that the house is a way station on the path from the forest down the hill to the sea.

LEFT | *Living large on the cliff face. With the 16-ft.-wide sliding doors fully open, the living space in the central cabin house flows out onto the terrace and embraces the water below.*

SITE PLAN

WATER'S EDGE

PREVAILING WINDS

From the landward approach side, the Olympic Mountains form a distant horizon, framed by one of the two gaps in the wall of the house.

In contrast to the exposed water-facing side, a more intimate space framed by a balcony above and bookshelves to the sides looks inward to the woods behind.

Framing the View

Inside the house, an amazing panorama spreads out to the south. Cutler wanted nothing to get in the way of the view, so he installed two massive wood and glass sliding doors on the south wall of the center cabin. The doors roll open majestically and allow the terrace outside under the broad overhang to become an extension of the living room—or perhaps it's the other way around.

In the same central cabin, a balcony on the landward side where the roof is higher shelters a smaller-scale sitting area below. This sitting area frames a view back into the forest. In houses on exposed sites that have such intense contact with the water, it's important to provide inward-looking spaces of retreat away from the view. The balcony

A pair of lofts to either side of the balcony provide a modicum of privacy but still remain connected to the action below.

overhead, reached via ships ladders that grow out of the bookshelves, is flanked by two small study lofts that give a further layer of separation but still leave the occupants connected to the communal space below.

A kitchen separated by an eating bar occupies the eastern end of the main floor space, balanced at the opposite end by a woodstove and couches for lounging. Although functions are separate within this central building, the spaces are integrated, just as they would be in a one-room cabin.

End Pieces

At either end under the connecting roof, smaller cabins house the parents' bedroom suite and the children's bedrooms and guest dormitory. The dormitory also has its own living space and mini-lofts, which serve as another place to escape to. The fact that you have to go outside to get to these other two cabins dramatically increases their privacy, and going back and forth reconnects you to the land and to the water. These more sheltered cabins are protected from winter storms by heavy doors that can be closed on the windward side, but there's still a strong sense of being out in the weather.

The kitchen anchors one end of the main space, with an eating bar and simple pot rack above marking a subtle separation of function.

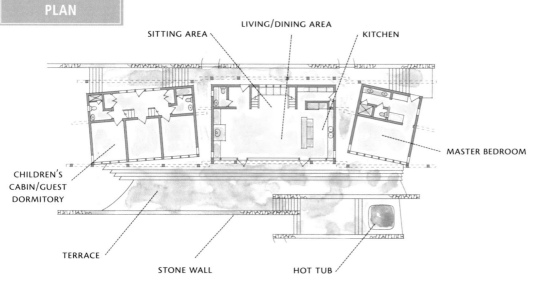

FIRST FLOOR PLAN

SITTING AREA

LIVING/DINING AREA

KITCHEN

MASTER BEDROOM

CHILDREN'S CABIN/GUEST DORMITORY

TERRACE

STONE WALL

HOT TUB

*With two lofts and a small downstairs living space, the dormitory cabin functions
almost independently from the main cabin.*

A Part of the Land

The need to withstand the high winds off the water and months of inclement weather was a major factor in the design of the house, but Cutler also needed to create a strong form to tie the building to the land on this powerful site. The tall, heavily braced north wall forms one support system for the sod roof, which is pitched down toward the water at the same low angle as the wind-blown trees. On the south side, a row of braced columns holds the roof up, and the cabins under this roof are largely independent of the structure. Below it all, a stone retaining wall forms a dam that keeps everything from slipping down the hill. Conceptually, it is the simplest of structures with the physical and visual strength to hold its own in this notch in the cliff.

ABOVE | *Like a mental imprint, reflections of the sea and mountains beyond are burned on the south-facing side of the house.*

BELOW | *Minimizing interior trim creates a delicate wall screen of windows, ensuring that the view through the bedroom windows is preserved.*

ABOVE | *Tall columns with diagonal bracing stand sentinel-like in front of the shingled wall, supporting the high end of the sod roof on the landward side of the house.*

FACING PAGE | *The overhang of the sod roof casts the house into shadow, making it blend with the rocks below.*

Under the sod roof and its massive underpinnings, things get a bit more complicated. The three cabins don't face the water head on but are slightly rotated. This orientation subtly changes the view from each building and makes the passages in between them narrow down on the waterside, which intensifies the experience as you approach the water. The change in angle also breaks up the reflections on the glass of the walls facing the ocean, which makes it a little more intriguing when seen from the water. You see glass, then the open spaces between the cabins, then more glass, but some of it is reflecting light and some of it isn't—and this entire facade is often in the shadow of the huge sod roof overhang.

Because the walls are hard for the eye to organize, you overlook them, concentrating instead on the line of the sod roof with its waving grass, the powerful vertical and diagonal lines of the columns, and the massive rock base, which blends with the cliff. The buildings underneath are gone, which was the architect's plan for this house in the first place. ✍

DETAILING TO FIT THE CONDITIONS

The hostile nature of the site placed some serious structural demands on this house. For one, the sod roof required some pretty beefy support to hold up its 250 tons. What appear to be cedar beams and columns are actually planks of wood and galvanized steel plates sandwiched together. This is a process called "flitching." Rather than hide this structural necessity, architect Jim Cutler made a statement with it. The steel flitch plates emerge from the columns where they need to be bigger for structural reasons, and the structure of the house comes alive.

The supports for the roof fall primarily outside the cabins sheltered below. This allows the structure to follow a logic dictated by engineering requirements and to be more suited to the larger scale of the landscape rather than the domestic scale inside the cabins.

The same flitching that's used in the structural frame shows up in the frames of the big doors and windows as well. Here, the steel plates protrude farther from the surrounding wood as they get closer to the middle of the opening. This is because they need to be deeper in the middle of the span to provide the bending strength to resist the wind pressure. Because of the strength of the steel, these flitch plates allow the beams and mullions of the glass wall to be small, and they also increase the sense of delicacy of the facade by adding breaks to the surfaces of the beams and mullions.

With a pitch that matches the angle of the trees that have been shaped by the prevailing winds, the sod roof captures the windswept nature of this challenging site.

Two side porches meet in a curved deck outside the living room. The pergola above provides shade from the high summer sun, while letting the lower winter sun into the house.

HUGGING THE SHORE

ARCHITECT PETER MANNING and his wife Susan had fond memories of summer vacations spent in shingled cottages along the Maine coast. When it came to designing their own house on the water on Bainbridge Island, Washington, it was only natural that they'd want to breathe a little Maine coast vernacular into their new home. The styles are mainly different in tone rather than substance, and the house they built is a thoroughly Pacific Northwest–based home.

The house hugs the shore, stepping down a south-facing hillside that ends in Port Orchard Narrows. It is on a street of tight lots, so fitting into the dense fabric of wooden houses and having the right relationship to the street are as important to its success as is its relationship to the water.

Tucked in along the shore, this house deftly weaves itself into the fabric of the neighboring wood houses, while at the same time remaining elegantly distinctive.

The framed openings in the gable wall above the entry, a device characteristic of Shingle-style buildings, allow light into the large window in the stair hall while still ensuring privacy on the second-floor balcony inside.

A Pause, Then Enter

From the street, the driveway opens onto a motor courtyard slightly below street level. The courtyard is framed by a lush shade garden, protected here from the sun and winds off the Narrows on the other side of the house. There is a great sense of arrival and repose, but the powerful form of the entrance gable asserts itself and draws you toward the front door.

The gable wall projects a few feet proud of the house and is punctuated by a screen of framed openings (see the photo at left). This device creates a sheltering enclosure over the front door, while at the same time allowing light to get through to the large windows in the wall of the house behind it. If the architect had brought the actual wall of the house out to this plane, it would have let in even more light but it would also have let anybody walking by on the street see inside the house. With this device, the owners get it all—protection over the porch, a welcoming entry, light inside, and privacy.

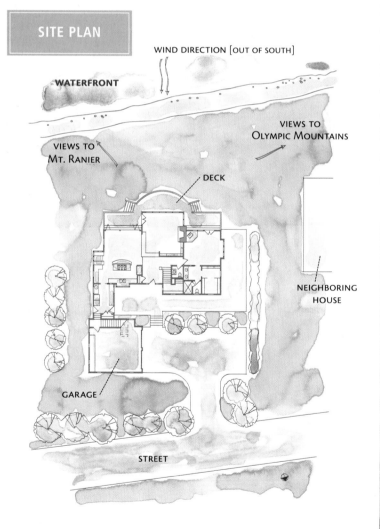

SITE PLAN

WIND DIRECTION [OUT OF SOUTH]

WATERFRONT

VIEWS TO
Mt. Ranier

VIEWS TO
Olympic Mountains

DECK

NEIGHBORING
HOUSE

GARAGE

STREET

The house steps down the hillside, hugging the grade and staying below the low height restriction mandated by local zoning. The fence marches alongside, in step and in style.

ABOVE | *The rich details and surfaces of the entry porch are a foretaste of the spectacular foyer inside.*

LEFT | *In contrast to the bright waterside exposure, the entry court is a shady oasis just below street level.*

Inside the foyer, the sweeping curve of the stair rail repeats the arch above the entry to the living room, while the small diamond inset tiles on the slate floor pick up the detailing on the newel post.

Fanning Out to the Water

The entry door opens onto a foyer with a grand curving staircase, which is the first indication of the richness that awaits throughout the house. The stair is like a big piece of furniture that graciously moves you upstairs, with steps big enough to lounge on, an inviting bench for sitting in the window, and a long wall of pictures. Stairs are always a chance to create a special moment in a house. Moving from floor to floor is the most processional movement in a house, and a good staircase doesn't rush you through it.

The foyer is the focal point for the entire house, and from this space the dining room and living room fan out toward the water. A fat Tuscan column functions as the pivot for two arches that create a sense of separation between the living room and the dining area and kitchen without blocking the view and the connection to the spaces and the water beyond. The combination of the arches and stepping down into the living room gives each space enough definition to be comfortable and cozy, but the connected view keeps things from getting claustrophobic.

A large Tuscan column, which echoes the columns at the entry porch, is a pivot point for two arches that define the boundaries of the living room.

WHAT STYLE IS IT?

This Pacific Northwest house has its roots in the Stick style and Queen Anne style that dominated architecture in the northeast from about 1860 to just past the turn of the last century.

Architect Peter Manning used elements from both these styles, but he also picked up the flavor of the woody architectural tradition in this region, where the strongest influence was the Craftsman style that began to gain sway in America as the Queen Anne style waned.

This house has the steep roofs, sharp edges, and angular qualities of the Stick style, but it also has some of the delicate trim typical in Queen Anne. The most distinctive exterior feature of this house is the broad overhang on the gable ends, which is characteristic of both Stick and Craftsman styles. But the way these gable overhangs are detailed with brackets and the omission of a decorative truss in the peak of the gable really points to the Craftsman style. The big overhangs also make sense in the rainy Pacific Northwest.

A covered porch one step down from the master bedroom is a great place for morning coffee. Having the porch here makes it easier to open up the room to the outside because the porch acts as a buffer, enhancing the sense of security on the inside.

One of two waterside porches on this house on Port Orchard Narrows, this porch is a bridge between inside and out—and a great alternative eating place just off the dining room.

Staying Intimate on the Water

On the first floor, the dining room, living room, and master bedroom command the best views of the water. The dining room and the bedroom both open onto covered porches on the water side, which eases the transition to the outside. From the outside, the porches frame windows and doors and create the rich pattern of light and shadow that makes this style of architecture so appealing. The two side porches merge into a semicircular deck with a pergola overhead that helps shade the living room from the high sun in the summer. Neither of these porches is large, but the grand gesture of the half-round central deck with its broad flight of stairs down into the garden makes the side porches feel intimate and welcoming.

From within the house, the views are framed with groups of traditional double-hung windows and hinged doors. There are no large expanses of glass because the owners wanted the feeling of enclosure brought by the smaller scale of windows with muntin bars. The effect is one of comfort rather than drama.

This effect is most pronounced in the living room, where the interior trim and details work together to re-create the kind of "at home" feeling that's reminiscent of a 19th-century cottage on the northeast coast. The arched entry, slightly higher

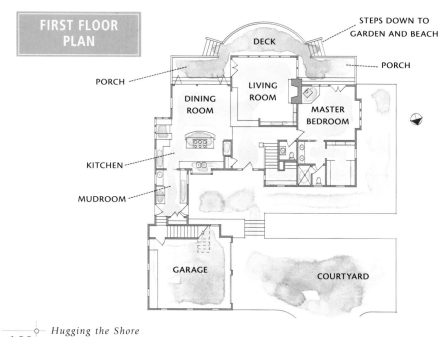

FIRST FLOOR PLAN

STEPS DOWN TO GARDEN AND BEACH

DECK

PORCH

PORCH

DINING ROOM

LIVING ROOM

MASTER BEDROOM

KITCHEN

MUDROOM

GARAGE

COURTYARD

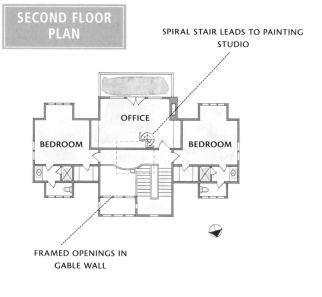

SECOND FLOOR PLAN

SPIRAL STAIR LEADS TO PAINTING STUDIO

OFFICE

BEDROOM

BEDROOM

FRAMED OPENINGS IN GABLE WALL

A bank of double-hung windows, each topped by a three-pane transom, frames the view out to the Narrows from the comfort of the living room.

ceiling (the room is one step down), and taller windows signify that this is the most important room in the house, while the textures of books in bookcases, natural trim framing views out to the Narrows, and the delicate stone and brick fireplace certainly make it the most comfortable.

Separate and Together

Both the owners work at home. Peter is a musician as well as an architect, and Susan is a painter. In a home in which two people work all day, it's important that there be separate spaces set aside for each person so they can work without distraction. Peter's office is over the garage, and he

Combining small pieces of granite, brick for the chimney, and a wood mantel creates a fireplace that's just the right scale for the room. The square opening reveals that this is a Rumford fireplace, one of the most efficient heaters.

Peter's office and music room looks down into the entry court (not shown) and out to the Narrows. The careful window composition throughout the house is continued in this space above the garage, with the larger foursquare window repeated at quarter size in the window with muntin bars beside it.

uses it for both work and music. Susan has arguably the best spot in the house (and certainly the highest)—a studio in the tower that is accessed from a spiral stair on the second floor.

When the work day is over, Peter and Susan like to cook together. With lots of space, no dead ends, and a massive center island, the kitchen is carefully laid out so that two people can work in the same space without running into each other. The kitchen also resolves the perennial problem of balancing the desire for a great view with the need for storage. All the essential storage is on the north and east walls (the landward side), which leaves the south side open to the other rooms and the water views beyond. ᔄ

ABOVE | *From the water side, the house is a symphony of windows and roof lines. The painting studio is the highest point in the house, visible above the second-floor gable.*

RIGHT | *Susan's painting tower, reached by a spiral stair, is the most private room in the house.*

ABOVE | *The massive center island, with casual seating, storage for books, and file drawers, is the center of activity for the homeowners, who love to cook together. There are no dead ends in the circulation pattern, which is a key for two people working in the same space.*

LEFT | *The breakfast nook in the southeast corner of the kitchen doubles as a spot for a quick snack and a place to pay bills (the kitchen island conveniently has a couple of file drawers built in).*

The west end of the house peers discreetly over the bushes, with the "comb" of the extended planks adding a dash of interest and echoing the lines of the rock escarpment.

THE ELEGANCE OF SIMPLICITY

IT'S A COMMON ENOUGH SCENE: A couple walk into an architect's office and tell the architect that they want a house that's simple, affordable, and won't be any trouble to maintain. Then they proceed to list all the things that they cannot possibly do without. This tiny lakeside house in northern Vermont is truly a house stripped bare to the essentials, but it's one that has stood the test of time due to the elegance of its design and the simplicity of its execution.

In 1969, Witold Rybczynski, who now has a wide reputation as an architecture critic, author, and teacher, was a few years out of architecture school when his parents asked him to design and build a summer house for them.

A small sitting porch and a diagonal entry ramp, the only element off the rectangular grid, welcome us to a house reduced to its essence.

The bedroom is separated from the main living space by a curtain not a wall, keeping the plan open and simple.

With a tight budget and only the summer to build it in, he knew he'd have to use some kind of prefab system. Rybczynski came across a cedar plank system from Pan Abode from western Canada (now located in the state of Washington), which uses stacked rows of tongue-and-groove planks that intersect at the corners like logs in a log cabin. For the plan of the house, he looked for inspiration to a house designed by Swiss architect Edouard Le Corbusier.

Afloat on the Site

The all-wood interior gives the house a dark, cavelike warmth, but it's not oppressive because the house is so small that you're always close to a window and the exterior view across the lake. In addition, the spaces are divided by curtains and corners rather than by walls and doors.

The all-wood technology allowed Rybczynski to save money by placing the building on concrete piers rather than on a continuous foundation wall. This would be risky in a conventional house finished with drywall or plaster, where any movement could cause cracking in the rigid wall finishes. Here, it not only saved money but also gives the house the appearance of floating above the site on a pool of shadow.

BUILDING ON HISTORY

The plan for this small cabin was inspired by a design the Swiss architect Le Corbusier did for his parents on Lake Lemano in 1925. A key element of that design was the open floor plan, which minimizes interior walls and doors and was one of the signatures of the then-new International style.

Interior corners are a problem with the plank-on-plank construction system because it demands that the wall planes cross each other at the corners, and these crossover ends are a bit clunky. Witold Rybczynski was looking for a design that would grow out of the technology rather than fight it, so the open plan idea made a great deal of sense. In Rybczynski's words, the result is a house in which "Mies van der Rohe meets Daniel Boone."

Hovering over its own shadow in a small grove of trees, the long low form of the house appears to float above the site.

Le Corbusier's plan paralleled the lakefront, but Rybczynski turned the house perpendicular to the lake to minimize the number of trees that would have to be cut down and to focus the living room more intensely on the lake. This siting decision also allowed him to set the house right on the edge of the escarpment, while lessening the visual impact of the house from the water. The front of the house with the entry doors faces an approach from the south, and the house itself forms the northern boundary of a small, protected exterior living space.

PARKING

CABIN

LAKE

Extending the wall and roof planes beyond the building emphasizes the horizontality of the house. The "combs" also serve as perfect filters for the late afternoon light on the lake.

Comb Walls

The plank-on-plank technology created an opportunity to extend the house outward at the exterior corners. By projecting the planks in one direction at the wall junctions, like the tines on a comb, the building appears to reach out to the site. Initially, Rybczynski had planned to combine the extended planks with boards overhead to create sunshades, but it turned out that these weren't necessary because the trees to the south provided sufficient shade. The extended planks now serve to remind us how this house fits together and bring an air of lightness as they filter the view of the lake.

Working with a classmate, Rybczynski built the house in a couple of weeks in the summer of 1969 at a material cost of under $5,000 (or about $25,000 in 2003 dollars). The current owner muses that he is planning to extend the deck along the south side, or maybe add a flight of stairs from there to a lower deck, or maybe . . . but the reality is that nobody has felt the need to significantly change this simple house for 35 years. ∽

FLOOR PLAN

BEDROOM

BEDROOM

KITCHEN

LIVING/DINING ROOM

DECK

COVERED PORCH   ENTRY

ABOVE | *Full-height windows in the living room focus the view on the lake. What little furniture there is in this almost monastic space is made out of leftover planks from the wall system.*

Look closely and you'll see the house perched on the clifftop, shrouded by pines on all sides. Very little of the natural environment was disturbed to make way for the house.

BALANCING ON THE EDGE

ALMOST A HUNDRED FEET ABOVE the Pacific Ocean, on the Mendocino County coast of northern California, architect Obie Bowman and his clients Pat and Peter have created a simple and elegant house that resides quietly in a grove of Bishop pines. The owners had strong ideas about the kind of house they wanted and how it would feel to be inside it. The balance between elegance and earthy rusticity is what drew them to this part of California, and they wanted the house to reflect this balance and at the same time have a simple plan.

Pat and Peter chose Obie Bowman to design their house because they liked the drama of his buildings, which often use striking design elements and spatial and scale changes to produce dramatic effects. They wanted a

Towering Ponderosa pine trunks trucked in from the Rockies form a four-posted entry foyer that changes the scale of the interior and brings light deep into the house.

The transparent corner of the living room merges with the sitting porch, creating a sheltered outdoor living space. The columns of the porch echo the surrounding pines.

FIRST FLOOR PLAN

BEDROOM

MASTER BEDROOM

SKYLIGHT ABOVE

LIVING ROOM

DINING AREA

PORCH

KITCHEN

more restrained house than he typically did, but not a boring one, and felt that a creative tension would result between Bowman's tendency toward dynamism and their own natural restraint.

Balancing the Light

Pat and Peter had lived on the water for many years, primarily in southern California, and they wanted both the protection from glare that a covered porch can bring and the ability to sit outside in inclement weather and watch the "moody" weather that this area is famous for. The north coast counties of California are often foggy, and houses surrounded with porches can be damp, dreary places when the sun never gets in. So the most compelling challenge for a house with wide porches is getting light inside.

Bowman designed wide sheltering porches on the south and west facing the water, and, to counteract the shading effect of the porch roof, he placed a skylight at the apex of the four hipped roof planes of the house. This skylight is over the entry foyer and brings light into the center of the house all day long. This light deep in the center of the house balances the more subdued light that comes in under the porch roof.

SITE PLAN

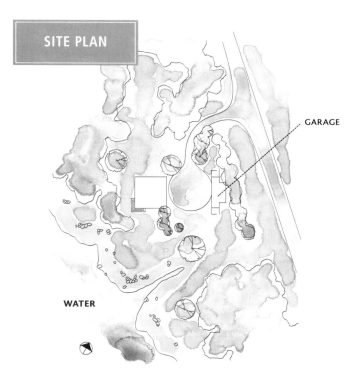

GARAGE

WATER

The porch roof itself is high enough that it doesn't block the view from most places inside the house, but it does exclude a big chunk of glare-producing sky. On the northwest corner, the master bedroom extends out into the porch space, breaking out of the square plan so that you can look south through the porch and down the coast as well as westward and out to sea. It's the only room in the house with views in three directions.

All of the living spaces are arranged around the perimeter and look out into the pine trees and the water views beyond. That outward focus is a counterpoint to the drama of the sunlight falling through the skylight in the center of the roof and splashing down the trunks of the giant ponderosa pines at the entry foyer. As a consequence of the balancing of these two different light sources and skillful window sizing, the house isn't dark, but it does feel sheltered, and as you move toward the perimeter everything seems resolved.

Extending the master bedroom out into the volume of the porch gives the owners a great view down the coast and involves the bedroom with the porch. It also projects the west-facing glass in this room out from under the porch to capture the Pacific sunsets.

Silhouetted against the evening sky, the simplicity and power of the roof shape stand in counterpoint to the rhythm of window and door openings marching along the south-facing porch.

Large-scale, repetitive window patterns draw the eye out to the view, while the simple dark ceiling and floor planes create a sense of repose.

Material Balance

Throughout the house, ceilings of Douglas fir recede into the shadows as the tentlike hipped roof gets higher. The patina of the recycled oak floors balances the soft brown shadows above. Sandwiched between these two warm-colored planes, the white walls and the windows in large simple rectangles generate a sense of calm. In this simple palette of colors and textures, elements like the rough stucco surface of the fireplace and the glistening "stump stools" take on a special presence and generate the touch of elegance Pat and Peter were looking for.

The tent roof that shapes the inside space makes a powerful form outside because of its focus on the central skylight. The shape of the hipped roof sliding out into the lower pitched roofs of the porches creates a simple, memorable image. This unity of shape gives a small house the presence to stand up to a powerful cliffside site without being either overwhelmed by it or competing with it.

LEFT | *The rough stucco surface of the fireplace and the glistening "stump stools" stand out against the simple palette of colors and repetitive window openings in the main living space.*

FACING PAGE | *The large skylight over the entry foyer balances the light coming in from the perimeter of the building. The foyer opens to every other room in the house.*

The low garage/ storage building serves as a screen between the road and the house, with only the top of the roof visible.

Raising the whirlpool tub to windowsill height gives bathers a great view of the ocean from this private clifftop site. The tub surround flows into the vanity countertop to create a seamless, unified design.

Public vs. Private

There's another set of tensions that has been balanced very nicely in this house. It is the tension of building a private house in a beautiful place that is in the public view. This house is an excellent example of client and architect upholding the public interest by building something that complements a beautiful landscape that the public has long admired and feels it "owns."

This house achieves this balance by following a few key principles. First, the size of the house is relative to the visual scale of the landscape. The large "executive estate" subdivision homes that are being built everywhere today are awkward not only because they are larger than they need to be but also because they sit on tiny lots like extra-large eggs in a medium-size carton. Here, the visual boundaries of the site are the edges of the promontory it sits on. As a result, the decision to build a house of only 1,400 sq. ft. was in scale with a piece of land that you comprehend in one glance.

BLENDING IN

Making a house murmur instead of shout takes a good deal of judgment that varies with each situation, but there are a few principles to keep in mind.

First, reflection can make a house shine like a beacon. Huge sheets of glass that aren't shaded by roofs can make a house leap into view. Although in certain cases reflecting the environment back to the viewer can make a sheet of glass very beautiful (as you can see in the top photo on p. 157), in most cases it doesn't help a house blend in. If there's a lot of glass, muntin bars can change the scale of the reflections but won't make them disappear. Shading the glass with big overhangs or porches is the best strategy.

Chameleon-like colors that make the house blend with the immediate environment are an obvious choice, but it's important to keep in mind what happens as the seasons change. Winter may not bring great differences in surrounding vegetation (as in the case of this house surrounded by pine trees), but it will greatly change the quality of light. Winter sun is lower in the sky and generally paler. Summer sun is higher and will pick up more of the surrounding colors. On sites where there are other houses nearby, it's more important to match the colors of those houses than that of vegetation if you want your house to blend in. In a land of weathered siding, painting a house any color will make it leap out.

Second, the house has an unobtrusive shape. Its simple, square form holds up well against the drama of this site, but it doesn't compete with it. By sitting comfortably in the site, it doesn't scream for attention. And third, the house uses sympathetic materials. With redwood board vertical siding and corrugated metal roofing, the exterior of the house runs from brown to silver-gray. It murmurs instead of shouting. From the beach below, all you can see is a corner of the roof and an occasional gleam of glass.

There will always be people who feel that it's an affront to build a house on such a spectacular site, but this house is designed with such restraint that it's hard to concede that it detracts from the setting. And once you've caught a glimpse of this house, it's hard to resist a quick pang of wishing you lived here. ⌒

A fanciful built-in storage unit in the master bedroom hides the large sliding wooden barn door that gives the bedroom privacy without cutting it off from the high light falling down into the central foyer.

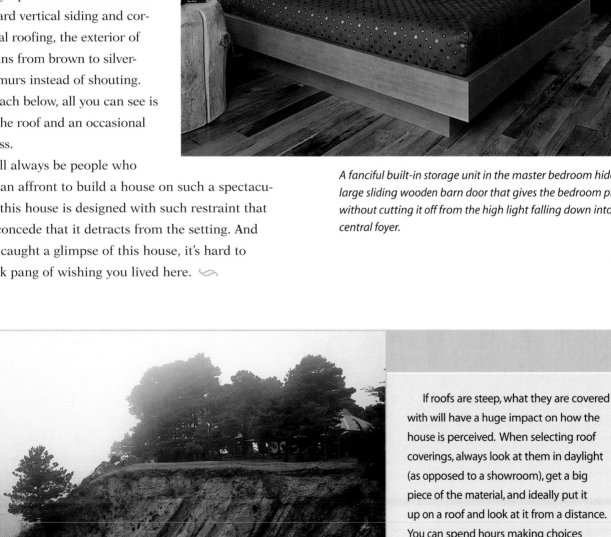

If roofs are steep, what they are covered with will have a huge impact on how the house is perceived. When selecting roof coverings, always look at them in daylight (as opposed to a showroom), get a big piece of the material, and ideally put it up on a roof and look at it from a distance. You can spend hours making choices using 2-in.-square shingle samples and be shocked at what they really look like on a roof.

When the sun hits just right, the house is visible from the river below. Half an hour later, it will disappear and blend into the backdrop of the trees.

A TENT ON THE RIVER

THE COUPLE WHO LIVE in this Connecticut River home had owned the land for many years, but they each had a different vision of the house they wanted to build there. The husband, a retired captain in the U.S. Navy who'd spent his life sailing the river, claimed that all he needed was a "tent on the river." Over the years, he'd watched plenty of large new houses sprout up along the river, and he didn't want his house to add to their number. Nor did he want the house to be visible from the yacht club below.

The captain's wife was looking for a little more than a tent. She'd always dreamed of a yellow-and-white house with a beautiful front entrance that would fit in with the houses in the village nearby. One thing the couple could

The entry foyer opens onto the main living space, where floor-to-ceiling windows give the illusion that you could step right out into the river.

ABOVE AND FACING PAGE (TOP) | *From the street, an arched opening leads into an entry court and from there to the front door. A square tower, or belvedere, anchors the tentlike roof and lets in light to the entry foyer below. At this point, there's no sense of the view that awaits on the other side of the door.*

agree on: They didn't want to waste any money on grand architectural statements. Theirs would be a small and efficient house—with a breathtaking view of the water.

A Four-Square Plan

Starting with the notion that the husband wanted a tent, architect Bill Grover of Centerbrook Architects designed a square-shaped house dominated by an umbrella-like roof that spreads out, over, and beyond the walls. A pair of strong diagonals—emphasized on the outside by the hips of the roof and on the inside by two large decorative trusses—intersect over the center of the entry foyer. The four-square layout puts a room in each corner of the plan. The captain gets a small bedroom with a corner view of the yacht club he founded (a view he initially said he didn't need but now appreciates). His wife's bedroom has only a partial view of the water but opens out onto a small walled garden that is her pride and joy.

Hanging over the Water

The main focus of the house is the living room and dining area, with the kitchen off to the side. In here, there's a sense of being in a canopied

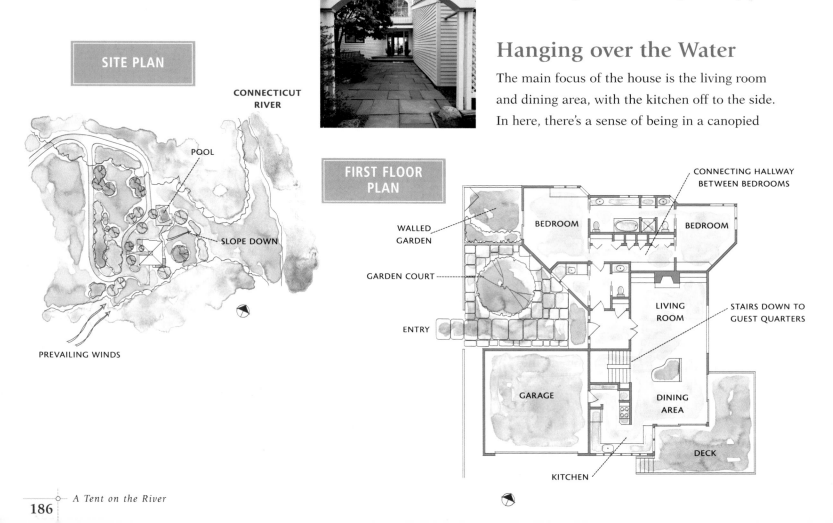

SITE PLAN

CONNECTICUT RIVER

POOL

SLOPE DOWN

PREVAILING WINDS

FIRST FLOOR PLAN

CONNECTING HALLWAY BETWEEN BEDROOMS

WALLED GARDEN

BEDROOM

BEDROOM

GARDEN COURT

LIVING ROOM

STAIRS DOWN TO GUEST QUARTERS

ENTRY

GARAGE

DINING AREA

DECK

KITCHEN

room, with the tentlike roof held up by the decorative trusses. But this room is about more than the tent; it's all about the view.

To get the full impact, it's best to follow the sequence of spaces from the street to the front door. Approaching from the driveway, first you go through an arched opening into a garden court that frames the view to the front door. From here, there's little suggestion of the river view beyond. As you enter the house, you get your first view of the river. Then stepping from the entry foyer into the living room, the river explodes into view (see the photo on p. 185). The wall is almost floor-to-ceiling glass and the land falls sharply away from grade at this point, so when you approach the river wall, it's almost as if the water is lapping at your feet.

Angled away from the water, this back bedroom opens out onto a small, fenced-in garden (visible at left). The window seat allows an oblique view to the river.

Narrow hallways between bedrooms can be dark and gloomy spaces, but here skylights above flood the hall with light, turning it into an interior room that is used for more than just coming and going between the two rooms.

The sharp drop in grade also allows another efficiency—putting all guest-related functions in the walkout basement, without it being a dark, gloomy space. The guests, mostly children and grandchildren, can stay down here in their own private world, which opens out onto the lawn. This lower level still has a view of the river, but it's more intimate (and safer for the grandchildren) than the high open deck above.

A Few Flourishes

Though the emphasis in this house is very much on efficiency, there are a couple of architectural flourishes in prominent spots where they can be fully appreciated and contribute to the comfort of the home. A tiny tower, or *belvedere*, centered above the entry foyer lets in light and ventilates the whole house by allowing warm air to flow up and out from the tentlike roof. The light falling down into the entry from the tower turns this into an enchanting space, an effect that is reinforced by the stained-glass front door panel and the colorful false relief painted into the floor tile.

The open, sloping ceilings of the tentlike roof make skylights particularly effective for bringing in light wherever it is wanted. For example, the hallway connecting the two

HOW TO HIDE A HOUSE

Some of us like a house on the water to stand out and make a statement. Others prefer that the house blend in. Architect Bill Grover was faced with the interesting challenge of making this Connecticut River home all but invisible from the water. Here's how he did it:

- By keeping the building horizontal, the house stays below the tree line and doesn't create a silhouette against the sky.

- Painting the base of the house dark brown makes the lower floor disappear, even in bright sunlight.

- The two sides visible from the water are painted a bark gray color, which is neutral in summer or winter. In summer, you can just see a light gray band, but in winter the color blends with the tree bark.

- By extending the roof overhang 6 ft. out on the water side, the upper gray portion is largely in shadow.

Decorative brackets support the tentlike roof over the main living space, making it feel as though you're standing under a giant sheltering canopy.

bedrooms is a wonderful interior room with lots of storage and space for family pictures, all made visible and useful by the sunlight flooding in from the skylights.

Executed with great understatement and simplicity, and with rooms laid out for the river view, this house effectively marries the competing visions that the owners had for their home, of a simple tent and a traditional clapboard town house. And though it's not quite invisible, it's about as close as you can get. ⌣

The stained-glass front door panel echoes the floor plan of the house and is itself reflected in the pattern of the screen door.

LEFT | *The wide, 6-ft. overhang creates a transition space from inside the house to the open deck—a sheltered spot that promotes easy movement from inside to out.*

FACING PAGE | *A small natural pool carved out of the ledge graces the north side of the property. The intentional imprint of the leaves in the concrete finish adds to the feeling that the pool grows out of the rock.*

Building the house into a steep hillside made it possible to incorporate a well-lit walkout basement, which serves as the guest quarters.

Standing tall in dappled sunlight, this house has a regal presence among the giant tulip poplar trees along this Maryland river.

A TALL HOUSE IN THE TREES

∾ **IT'S INTERESTING TO COMPARE** two different houses in similar waterfront settings to see how each house responds to specific site conditions. It's even more interesting when both houses are by the same architect. Earlier, we looked at a house designed by Peter Bohlin on a wooded lakeside site in Montana (see pp. 100–107). That house hugged low to the ground so that it wouldn't compete with the site—and did it so successfully that you hardly know it's there. By contrast, this house, on a forested site overlooking a river that flows into Chesapeake Bay, soars three stories high into a canopy of giant tulip poplar trees.

From the beginning, Bohlin (of Bohlin Cywinski Jackson) envisioned a strong vertical structure for the house, reasoning that moving vertically

The tiny window up top makes the door seem larger, a manipulation of scale that creates a more inviting entry.

Because the entry is separate from the main building, there's room for a grander stairway than you would expect on this small footprint. The stair run goes straight up from the entry to the third floor.

through the house would enhance the sense of being at the water's edge, with the view changing as you climbed the stairs. He also knew that a taller building would require a smaller footprint, meaning that fewer trees would have to be cut down. Finally, the house needed height to hold its own in the grove of poplars, making the house blend comfortably with its surroundings while providing shimmering glimpses of the river between the tree trunks.

A Cottage Entry

The powerful vertical form that works so well from the water needed a different face to pull us in as we approach by land. At the foot of the path down the hill, a small gable-roofed entry pavilion is set off at an angle from the main body of the house. With a tiny window up high and a slightly oversized door in this diminutive facade, the scale of the building is brought down to people size. Like Hansel and Gretel's fairytale cottage, it imparts a welcome sense of arrival home in the forest.

Using a separate structure for the entry, which is built a few steps above the ground-floor level of the house, allowed Bohlin to pull the first-to-second floor staircase outside the shell of the main building, thereby giving it a bit more grace and size as befits the main stair in a vertically oriented house.

WHAT STYLE IS IT?

Designed in the mid-1980s, at the height of what the media has dubbed the "Postmodern" style, this house represents the best of an era when architects experimented with new ways of thinking about design.

Beginning in the late 1960s, Postmodern architects used humor and changes of scale to make buildings more expressive than would have been deemed proper a generation before. Though some of these buildings look silly today (particularly those that were "style" driven), the good ones remain relevant because their creators relied on their instincts about the proper use of space, form, and motion, which is how good buildings have always been designed. Good design becomes classic, regardless of the era it lives in.

ABOVE | *The casual living room has two points of focus: the fireplace at the core of the house and the view of the water at the opposite end. The column to the right of the fireplace is the center point from which the four ground-floor rooms radiate.*

LEFT | *From the kitchen, a long-distance view leads through the breakfast nook in the glass tower to the river beyond. In a plan with few walls, rooms are separated by framed openings and inlays on the floor.*

The Core of the House

On all three floors, modest-sized rooms are grouped around the vertical spine of the chimney, creating the feeling of being inside a tree house or, better yet, inside the tree itself. On the ground floor, the living room, breakfast nook, and kitchen pivot on a slightly oversized Doric column that echoes a huge column on the front porch. These three rooms all have views to the river, while the dining room looks back into the forest and at the hearth in the center of the house. In contrast to the free-flowing spaces facing the water, the dining room is quiet and contemplative, sheltering under a low ceiling on the west side of the house.

Climbing Up through the House

On the second floor, the master bedroom, like the dining room below it, is a quieter space tucked back into the forest and away from the commanding views of the water. In houses that have long-distance views, it's desirable to have a few more confined and internal spaces for relief, especially in rooms used for quiet activities like sleeping and studying.

ABOVE | *Like the dining room below it, the master bedroom looks back into the trees, trading the drama of the water views for the sheltering security of the forest. The open beams, built-in furniture, and large posts on the bed enhance the sense of enclosure and comfort.*

FACING PAGE | *The dining room drops down a couple of steps from the entry and is sheltered beneath a low exposed ceiling, a quiet retreat from the more dramatic views over the water from the living room and kitchen.*

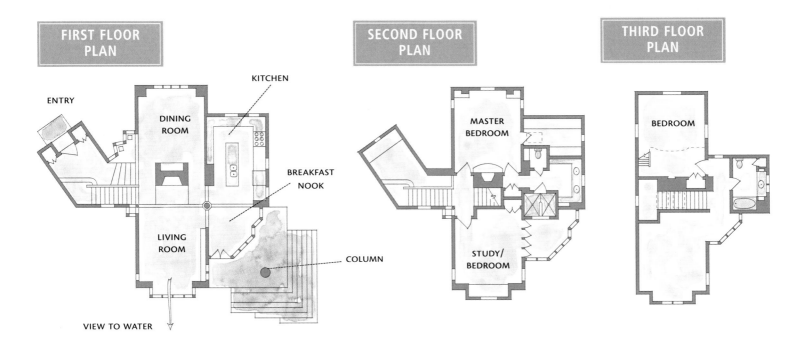

FIRST FLOOR PLAN

ENTRY

DINING ROOM

KITCHEN

BREAKFAST NOOK

LIVING ROOM

COLUMN

VIEW TO WATER

SECOND FLOOR PLAN

MASTER BEDROOM

STUDY/ BEDROOM

THIRD FLOOR PLAN

BEDROOM

The other bedroom on this floor looks out at the water to the east but also into the glass tower on the northern side. With glass opening onto the stair as well, this room feels suspended between pools of light and has a more transitory feeling than the quiet bedroom in the back.

As you continue to climb up through this house, the world outside the windows changes much more than it would if the house was spread out along the ground. You can see farther, and you start looking down on the river rather than out at it. All through the house there are chances not only to look out at framed views of the water but also to look up and down within the house itself—

LEFT | *With a stair wall that turns into a window and four large casement windows that open into the glass tower, this second-floor bedroom feels like it's suspended in space.*

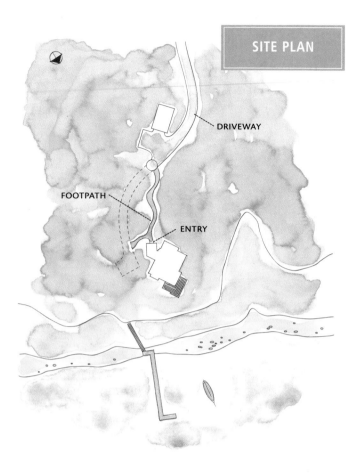

DRIVEWAY

FOOTPATH

ENTRY

The zigzag glass wall on the entry side is a small-scale version of the soaring glass tower on the water side. The wall brings light into the darker side of the house and provides an elegant connection between the entry building and the main house.

into the glass tower from the bedrooms and back into the staircase.

Interior windows (the architectural term is "borrowed lights") add an element of fun as well as remind us of the vertical organization controlling the design. As we climb through the house the rooms become more discreet, befitting their purpose of bathing or sleeping or studying, but because of the borrowed lights and glimpses of the ever-present stairway at the core, we are subtly reminded and reassured of the formal order at the heart of the design.

Zigzag Window Walls

Back on the outside, the zigzag walls of windows on the entry side and the water side serve a couple of different purposes. Because the little entry building connects to the main house at an acute angle some kind of transition is needed to deal with this awkward connection. Putting a flat wall with a window in it would look pasted on and diminish the separateness of the entry space. This accordion-like wall of glass makes the wall plane disappear and serves both to provide a glimpse inside and to bring a great deal of diffused north light into the darker side of the house.

On the other side of the house, the same device creates a three-story-high wall of glass that almost all the rooms look into. This vertical light and air shaft connects all three floors, echoing in light and volume the masonry spine nearby. The zigzag pattern of the wall gives it the strength to be three stories tall and allows it to work like one big window, but the breaks in the plane and the smaller "lights" in the window don't make it seem crushingly huge. It's one more example of how Bohlin's skill at manipulating scale and space makes this house at the water's edge such a wonderfully comfortable place to live.

Interior windows (called "borrowed lights") and shuttered openings into the stairwell let light from skylights above flood into this bedroom tucked under the roof on the third floor.

ABOVE AND LEFT | *The three-story glass tower creates a strong vertical link between floors. On the outside, the wall of windows and the corner column change the scale of the tall building and introduce a playful element that's emblematic of the Postmodern style.*

BELOW | *Moving horizontally through a house doesn't change your perspective of the water much, but moving vertically does. Up on the third floor, the house is tall enough to be up in the forest canopy and views are down to the river rather than out to it.*

The separate parts of this cottage, tied together by roofs and pergola, exude a quiet confidence and a sense of belonging to this site sheltered behind the guardian sand dunes.

THE COTTAGE AND THE CAMP

ON MARTHA'S VINEYARD'S WINDSWEPT north shore, a picturesque cottage with a settled air nestles behind a barrier of protective sand dunes. Less than a mile up the road, a compact "camp" floats alone above a sea of dune grass. The two beachfront houses are roughly the same size (about 1,500 sq. ft.) and were both designed by architect Phil Regan of Mark Hutker Associates, but they each use a different design strategy to fit into the same landscape. Let's take a look at the Cottage first.

The white trim, grey shingles, dormers, and chimneys are reminiscent of countless shorefront homes. By skillfully balancing and composing these elements, the architect has created a house that is inviting, reassuring, and human-scaled.

On the approach from the beach, the long line of the pergola ties the elements of the house together and settles it in place. It almost seems as though the house was here first and the dunes have sprung up around it.

SITE PLAN

OCEAN

DRIVEWAY

The Cottage: Hiding in the Vernacular

Regan's first priority was to minimize the Cottage's impact on the neighboring houses. The building is in the foreground view of a number of neighbors higher inland, and the architect was concerned about how the cottage would appear from the land side.

The "story and a half" design is a variation of countless New England vernacular cottages, and, as a result, it's what you expect to see along the shores of this island. While the arrangement of space inside the building and the actual spaces themselves are more contemporary in spirit, the house succeeds in becoming invisible by seeming to be typical. It takes on the apparent coloration and shape of many houses along these shores. So, even though the bright white trim stands out against the gray shingle, because you are so used to it in this environment, it doesn't stand out.

Traditional Rooms

The Cottage has the feel of a traditional home in that, from the outside, it seems to be composed of "rooms" rather than one large combined living space. You can sense those separate pieces in the way dormers poke out of the roof and in the many corners that seem to define rooms within.

Moving the French doors inside the exterior line of the building recesses and protects the door from the elements. At the same time, the entry side wall forms the end of the window seat, creating a subtle sense of enclosure for the living room part of this combined space.

An all-wood white painted interior simplifies the built-in cabinetry so the room doesn't become too fussy and the view outside can maintain its strong presence.

The upstairs hall is just wide enough to accommodate an alternative "napping room" outside the master bedroom, where a daybed can be used for overflow guests or noisy partners.

Wainscoting, wooden shutters, exposed ceiling, and claw-foot tub work together to fulfill our expectations of the quintessential beach house bathroom.

These visible pieces fitting together change the scale of the exterior, making it seem smaller and cozier. It's the kind of house that you want to go inside and explore, to see if it's really as it seems.

Once inside, the Cottage is surprisingly open, with a combined living room, dining area, and kitchen looking out on wide-angle views of the ocean. But a screened porch that projects into this unified space helps define separate functional areas. Varying the ceiling height and insetting the French doors on both the entry and the water side in the middle of the space creates enough of an edge that the living room has its own sense of place and the traditional furniture grouping feels right at home.

Upstairs, a bedroom, a bathroom, and a sitting area hunker down under a low-pitched roof. All the rooms have a view over the dunes to the water, but the low roof overhead reassuringly emphasizes the job the building is doing of protecting you from the elements. Leaving the rafters exposed makes the low roof less oppressive, and in the bedroom the trim line carried around at windowsill height creates a scale change that makes the room feel smaller and cozier. The highly practical "napping room" at the top of the stairs is really just a space enlarged out of the upper stair hall, but even without the great water view it feels like a fine place to curl up in.

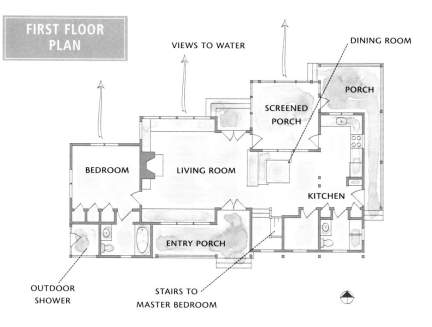

FIRST FLOOR PLAN

VIEWS TO WATER

DINING ROOM

PORCH

SCREENED PORCH

BEDROOM   LIVING ROOM

KITCHEN

ENTRY PORCH

OUTDOOR SHOWER

STAIRS TO MASTER BEDROOM

With exposed rafters under a low roof and chair-rail trim at mid-height, there's a wonderful sense of cozy containment in the upstairs master bedroom. The double-hung windows drop down low to provide a view of the ocean beyond the dunes.

The screened-porch dining room (with glass inserts for cooler fall days) gets you right out into the dunes on the north side of the cottage.

Inside Out, Outside In

For a relatively small house, the Cottage has more than its share of inside-outside transition spaces. The screened porch, which can be reached from both the living room and the kitchen, is used for "outdoor" dining when the weather is right. Just beyond the barely contained feeling of the screened porch, an open porch on the northwest corner takes the next step to the outside, with just a hint of shelter from a pergola above. And from there the sand is just a step away.

The pergola on the southern side of the living room creates an inviting front porch without shading the living room as a solid roof would. It also helps make the window seat inside the living room feel much more protected by framing the view and giving someone sitting there a sense of another layer to the building beyond the glass. On the water side to the north, yet another pergola breaks up the high wall of glass and creates a long horizontal element that ties this whole side of the house together.

This masterful use of pergolas and transition spaces emphasizes the human scale of the house, making it seem comfortable and in exactly the right place. The overall impression is of a cottage settling down into the dunes and beach roses like a dog walking in a circle then lying down in tall grass.

ABOVE | *With the sand just a step away, this deck has just a hint of protection provided by the pergola above.*

RIGHT | *A pergola on the north side toward the water serves as a unifying horizontal element along the facade and creates a transition zone that encourages those on the inside to venture out. The screened porch is to the left of the steps.*

A pergola over the entry porch provides a sense of enclosure and protection without shading the living room windows beyond. Inside, the window seat is wide enough to double as a place to sleep, and the drawers below provide extra storage.

In contrast to the cottage, which hunkers down in the dunes, the Camp floats proudly above them.

SITE PLAN

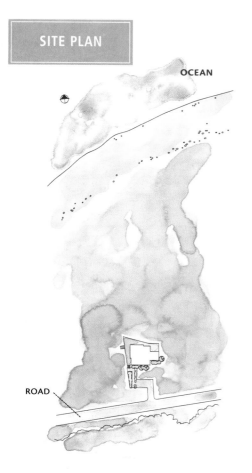

OCEAN

ROAD

The Camp: Out in the Action

A few hundred yards up the road, Regan needed to use a different strategy to make the Camp fit in. Regan had the same concerns about the impact of the house on the view of the neighbors inland, but he knew he wouldn't be successful using the Cottage strategy of hiding it in vernacular clothes because he couldn't keep the building down at sand level.

To comply with local zoning, the Camp had to be built within the "footprint" (the area on the ground) of an existing fisherman's shack, so the maximum size and location of the building were predetermined. Floodplain restrictions further required that the first floor be raised about 5 ft. above grade. Putting a house like the Cottage at this height would have made it look like a fish out of water. So Regan opted for a single-story building to minimize the overall height and still allow for the high sloping ceilings that would give a spacious feeling inside.

RIGHT | *Although the building is only one-story high, the vaulted ceiling and wall of windows with clerestory above opening to the view make the main living room seem much larger than its modest dimensions.*

LEFT | *By breaking the house down into two pavilions, the overall height of the building was made lower. The pavilion at right, the smaller of the two, encloses the master bedroom.*

BELOW | *Massing the windows in the corner opens the master bedroom to the ocean view and emphasizes the diagonal in the room, making it seem a bit more spacious. Dropping the window sills lower at the foot of the bed allows a wider view, while the beadboard paneling around the bed gives a greater sense of enclosure where it's needed.*

The main room, with a kitchen tucked into one side, a vaulted ceiling, and white painted beadboard interiors, is the essence of beach casual. Nobody has to dress for dinner here.

Divide and Lower

Regan further minimized the height of the building by dividing the house into two pavilions with low-pitched hipped roofs connected by a section of flat roof. This design meant that the length of the slope of each roof was shorter, and, consequently, the roof peaks are not as high as they would have been if a single roof covered the entire floor plan.

A "camp" should be a casual, simple place to live—and this building fits that description to a tee, with one big combined living-eating-cooking space under the larger pavilion to the west. At the other end of the house, the master bedroom occupies the mini-pavilion and is connected back to the main living space by the expansive wraparound deck outside. Surprisingly for such a small house, there's also room for three other bedrooms and three baths neatly fitted in around the main space under flat roofs on the south and east. Though none of the bedrooms is large, the fact that they are all located on corners

with windows on two sides gives them a nice airy quality that belies their size. Throughout the house, built-in furniture maximizes use of space, serving to move the Camp into a world that is more like a boat than a regular house.

Turning Problems into Opportunities

On the exterior, Regan used bands of vertical boarding, shingles, and horizontal boarding so the house appears to be a stack of narrower layers. The horizontality introduced by this layering reinforces the feeling that the house is hovering over its base. The lower layer of shingles, which runs between the windowsills and the concrete pylon foundation, flares slightly where it meets the pylons and then changes to boards. The pylons need to protrude beyond the wall of the house for engineering reasons. Instead of trying to hide this necessity, the architect made it work to his

advantage with an elegant detail that makes the building seem to float even more lightly over its base.

This entire house is a good example of how an architect can turn a problem imposed by being on the water into a visual advantage. Rather than struggle against the need to put the house up in the air on concrete pillars, Regan made the elevation of the first floor above the surrounding land the essence of the design, and then responded with appropriate shapes and detailing so the house overcomes the practical problem. As a result, being elevated seems aesthetically desirable rather than simply a practical solution.

Chameleon Colors

On the Cottage, the white trim and gray shingles are unobtrusive because they fit our expectations of what should be on that vernacular house in that protected location. If the same colors had been used on the Camp, elevated above the dunes, the effect would have been strikingly different and the building would have shouted for attention. By staining the trim, shingles, and vertical siding with bleaching oil to bring out the natural gray and doors and win-

In a small house, every inch counts. This built-in bureau uses space wisely and emphasizes the boat-like quality of the house.

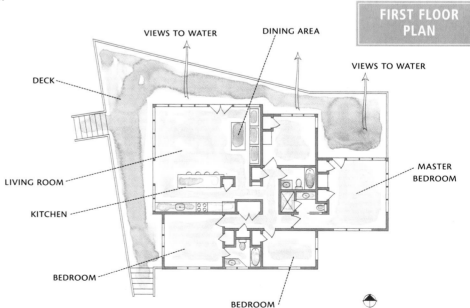

ABOVE | *A single light of glass in a traditional six-over-one window allows an uninterrupted view to the water.*

LEFT | *Dividing the exterior siding into layers of different materials creates a more horizontal composition that makes the building seem to hover over the posts below it.*

KNOW THE FLOODPLAIN

One of the biggest challenges of building a house on the water is the threat that one day the house could be *under* water. This is why it is critical to know the disposition of the floodplain on any coastal property that you buy.

The floodplain is defined as the area that would be covered by water in what engineers calculate to be a flood that has a statistical likelihood of happening once in 100 years. The government has mapped most of the floodplains of the United States and has distributed these maps to local jurisdictions that describe the extent of the statistical 100-year flood.

If your site is actually in the floodplain, your architect will have to design it according to regulations published by the Federal Emergency Management Agency, or you will be ineligible for flood insurance, and hence probably ineligible for a mortgage. And, of course, if you are in the floodplain, you'll probably want that insurance.

The heavy concrete pylons and open structure of the building shown here is the kind of design that is mandated for "velocity zones," those areas of the floodplain where wave action is expected to occur. This is the most rugged design level required. Here, the boards behind the concrete pylons are designed to break away and let the waves wash through.

In any part of the flood zone, all living areas are required to be 1 ft. to 2 ft. above the height of the theoretical flood. In the case of the Camp, the government figured that waves at least 5 ft. high could be rolling over this site during the "big one."

ABOVE | *Seen from the beach at dusk, the two pavilions huddle together in this exposed location to create a more welcoming, less obtrusive facade than would be presented by a single monolithic structure.*

FACING PAGE | *The deck railing is a simple wood frame with thin stainless-steel cables that make it almost invisible, complementing the exterior of the building, which is without any noticeable adornment.*

dows with the color "sand," the colors match the tones of the surrounding sand and flora and the building blends in.

Other outside elements of the house also minimize visual impact. The deck railing is a simple frame with thin stainless-steel cables that make it almost invisible, and the exterior of the building is without any real adornment to catch the eye. Rather than the rich display of transition spaces and elements like pergolas that Regan used so successfully on the Cottage, this small building revels in a sharp transition from inside the shelter to being out in the wind, under the sky as if you were on the deck of a boat.

Responding to the Site

These two buildings on Martha's Vineyard are a textbook study of how architectural responses grow out of the site. The two sites are less than a mile apart and the two houses are similar in size, but each building required a different response to the site.

Zoning rules allowed the architect to design the Cottage close to grade, and he was able to create the kind of beach-front living where you can feel the sand between your toes. When site constraints on the Camp's piece of beach front wouldn't allow that, he responded with a building that makes us forget about that contact with the ground and revels in floating above the dunes looking out to sea. And, above it all, both are still good neighbors for the houses behind them. ⌣

ARCHITECTS, DESIGNERS, and BUILDERS

A Quiet Fit *(pp. 20–27)*
Estes/Twombly Architects, 79 Thames
St., Newport, RI 02840
www.estestwombly.com

design team: Jim Estes, designer;
Robin Linhares, project manager;
contractor: Wes Dean, Highland Builders,
Tiverton, RI

**Between the Garden and
the Bay** *(pp. 28–35)*
Cass Calder Smith Architects,
44 McLea Court, San Francisco,
CA 94103
www.ccs-architecture.com

design team: Cass Calder Smith, design
principal; Ian Glidden, Alex Chiapetta;
landscape architect: Brad Burke, San
Francisco, CA; *structural engineer:* John
Yadeger Associates, San Francisco, CA;
contractor: Werner Schneider
Construction, Tiburon, CA

The Perfect Site *(pp. 36–43)*
Knight Associates, Architects,
P.O. Box 803, Blue Hill, ME 04614
www.knightarchitect.com

design team: Robert Knight, design principal; Peter d'Entremont, project manager;
contractor: Michael Hewes, Blue Hill, ME

The Sand between Your Toes
(pp. 44–51)
Techler Design Group, 11 Boyd St.,
Watertown, MA 02472
www.techlerdesign.com

design team: Timothy Techler, AIA, design
principal; Scott Engstrom, Jason Roan;
landscape architect: Reed/Hilderbrand
Associates, Watertown, MA; *contractor:*
YFI Custom Homes, Cape Neddick, ME

Resurrecting a Lakeside Bungalow
(pp. 52–61)

design team: Kurt and Sally Rivard, with:
contractor: Philip and MaryVi White,
Hartford, Wis.

A House over the Water *(pp. 62–69)*
Jacobson Silverstein Winslow
Architects, 3106 Shattuck Ave.,
Berkeley, CA 94705
www.jswarch.com

design team: Max Jacobson, partner in
charge; *contractor:* Lou Fox, Davis, CA

A House of Many Faces *(pp. 70–77)*
Roc Caivano Architects, 38 Rodick St.,
Bar Harbor, ME 04609
www.roccaivanoarchitects.com

design team: Roc Caivano, principal
designer; Robert Willis, Matt Carter;
contractor: John Follis, Swan's Island, ME

Where Porch Is King *(pp. 78–83)*
Historical Concepts, Inc.,
430 Prime Point, Suite 103, Peachtree
City, GA 30269
www.historicalconcepts.com

design team: Jim Strickland, design prin-
cipal; Terry Pylant, David Bryant, Jeff
Morrison, the late Phillip Windsor;
landscape architect: Donald Hooten,
Decatur, GA; *contractor:* H. L. Griffin
Builder, Savannah, GA

Preserving Privacy in a Public Place *(pp. 84–91)*
Glen Irani, Architects, 410 Sherman Canal, Venice, CA 90291

design team: Glen Irani, design principal; *structural engineer:* Pugh + Scarpa, Santa Monica, CA; *contractor:* Irani/Projects

A Sense of Scale *(pp. 92–99)*
Stephen G. Smith, Architects, Harbor Square, P.O. Box 726, Camden, ME 04843
www.sgsmitharchitects.com

design team: Stephen Smith, AIA; *contractor:* Bruce Laukka, West Rockport, ME

The Elements of Style *(pp. 100–107)*
Bohlin Cywinski Jackson, 1932 First Ave., Suite 916, Seattle, WA 98101
www.bcj.com

design team: Peter Q. Bohlin, FAIA, principal-in-charge; Steve Mongillo, AIA, project manager; *landscape architect:* Swift and Company; *structural engineer:* Beaudette Consulting Engineers; *contractor:* Martel Construction

A Roof on the Ridge *(pp. 108–115)*
John Silverio, Architect, Proctor Rd., RR1 Box 4725, Lincolnville Center, ME 04859

design team: John Silverio, design principal; *landscaping:* Sue Hatch; *stone walls:* Fred Porter; *contractor:* Robert Clayton, Islesboro, ME

Living Out on the Lake *(pp. 116–123)*
Daniel V. Scully, Architects, 17 Elm St., Keene, NH 03431
www.scully-architects.com

design team: Daniel Scully, with Susan Phillips-Hungerford; *landscape architect:* Saucier and Flynn; *structural engineer:* Richard Keller; *contractor:* Richard Pisciotta, Builder, Peterborough, NH

Industrial Strength *(pp. 124–131)*
Balance Associates, Architects, 101 Euclid Ave., Seattle, WA 98122
www.balanceassociates.com

design team: Tom Lenchek, AIA, and Marcus Schott; *structural engineer:* Jay Taylor, Skilling, Ward, Magnusson, and Barkshire, Seattle, WA
contractor: Precision Builders, Des Moines, WA

Standing Alone *(pp. 132–139)*
Shim-Sutcliffe Architects, 441 Queen St. East, Toronto, Ontario, M5A 1T5;

design team: Brigitte Shim and Howard Sutcliffe, design principals; Donald Chong, Jason Emery Groen, Andrew Chatham, John O'Connor; *structural engineer:* Aitkins + Van Groll Engineers; *contractor:* Judges Contracting; *millwork:* Steve Bugler, Radiant City Millwork; *custom fabrication:* Takashi Sakamoto

A Question of Balance *(pp. 140–149)*
Knight Associates, Architects, P.O. Box 803, Blue Hill, ME 04614
www.knightarchitect.com

design team: Robert Knight, design principal; Peter d'Entremont, project manager; *contractor:* Michael Hewes, Blue Hill, ME

Grace Notes (pp. 150–159)
Cutler Anderson Architects, 135 Parfitt
Way SW, Bainbridge Island, WA 98110
www.cutler-anderson.com

design team: James Cutler, design
principal; Janet Longnecker,
project architect; Julie Cripe;
contractor: Russett Construction,
Lopez Island, WA

Hugging the Shore *(pp. 160–169)*
Manning Architecture and Planning,
9811 South Beach Dr., P.O. Box 11746,
Bainbridge Island, WA 98110

design team: Peter C. Manning, AIA, project
principal; Susan B. Manning, interior
design; *structural engineer:* Paul Faget,
Swenson Say Fagét, Seattle, Wash.; *contractor:* Monte Hall Construction, Bainbridge
Island, WA

The Elegance of Simplicity
(pp. 170–175)
Witold Rybczynski, Architect; *contractor:* Witold Rybczynski and Ralph
Bergman, using a kit made by Pan
Abode Cedar Homes, Renton, WA

Balancing on the Edge *(pp. 176–183)*
Obie G. Bowman Architect,
9811 South Beach Dr., P.O. Box 1114,
Healdsburg, CA 95448
www.sonic.net/~ogb/

design team: Obie G. Bowman, AIA,
design principal; Rob Heaney, David
Arkin, Mike Cobb; *contractor:* Helmut
Emke Custom Builders, Gualala, CA

A Tent on the River (pp. 184–191)
Centerbrook Architects and Planners,
P.O. Box 955, Centerbrook, CT 06409
www.centerbrook.com

design team: William H. Grover, FAIA,
design principal; Stephen L. Lloyd,
project manager; *contractor:* Post Road
Wood Products, CT

A Tall House in the Trees
(pp. 192–199)
Bohlin Cywinski Jackson,
8 West Market St., Suite 1200,
Wilkes-Barre, PA 18701
www.bcj.com

design team: Peter Q. Bohlin, FAIA,
principal-in-charge; Margaret E. Bakker,
AIA, project manager; Anthony Childs,
interior design; *landscape architect:* John P.
Gutting; *structural engineer:* Utility
Engineers; *contractor:* Berliner
Construction

The Cottage and the Camp
(pp. 200–215)
Mark Hutker and Associates,
Architects, P.O. Box 2347, Tisbury
Market Place, Beach Rd., Vineyard
Haven, MA 02568
www.hutkerarchitects.com

design team: Phil Regan, project architect,
with Carol Hunter; *contractor:* Serpa
Brothers Construction, Edgartown, MA
(Cottage); Johnson Builders, West
Tisbury, MA (Camp)